VLADIMIR ILICH LENIN

VLADIMIR ILICH LENIN

John Haney

CHELSEA HOUSE PUBLISHERS
NEW YORK
NEW HAVEN   PHILADELPHIA

EDITOR-IN-CHIEF: Nancy Toff
EXECUTIVE EDITOR: Remmel T. Nunn
MANAGING EDITOR: Karyn Gullen Browne
COPY CHIEF: Juliann Barbato
PICTURE EDITOR: Adrian G. Allen
ART DIRECTOR: Giannella Garrett
MANUFACTURING MANAGER: Gerald Levine

Staff for LENIN:

SENIOR EDITOR: John W. Selfridge
COPY EDITORS: James Guiry, Karen Hammonds
EDITORIAL ASSISTANT: Sean Ginty
ASSOCIATE PICTURE EDITOR: Juliette Dickstein
PICTURE RESEARCHER: Lisa Kirchner
SENIOR DESIGNER: David Murray
ASSISTANT DESIGNER: Jill Goldreyer
PRODUCTION COORDINATOR: Joseph Romano
COVER ILLUSTRATION: Alan J. Nahigian

CREATIVE DIRECTOR: Harold Steinberg

First Printing

1 3 5 7 9 8 6 4 2

Library of Congress Cataloging in Publication Data

Haney, John D.
  Vladimir Ilich Lenin / John Haney.

    p.   cm.—(World leaders past & present)
Bibliography: p.
Includes index.
  Summary: Follows the life of the leader of the Bolshevik Revolution, who
became the first head of the Soviet state.
  ISBN 0-87754-570-7
1. Lenin, Vladimir Ilich, 1870–1924—Juvenile literature.
2. Statesmen—Soviet Union—Biography—Juvenile
literature. 3. Soviet Union—History—20th century—Juvenile
literature. [1. Lenin, Vladimir Ilich, 1870–1924. 2. Heads of
state. 3. Revolutionists. 4. Soviet Union—History—20th
century.] I. Title. II. Series.
DK254.L455H36   1988   947.084′1′0924—dc 19 [B] [92]
87-26584   CIP   AC

Chronology

John Adams
John Quincy Adams
Konrad Adenauer
Alexander the Great
Salvador Allende
Marc Antony
Corazon Aquino
Yasir Arafat
King Arthur
Hafez al-Assad
Kemal Atatürk
Attila
Clement Attlee
Augustus Caesar
Menachem Begin
David Ben-Gurion
Otto von Bismarck
Léon Blum
Simon Bolívar
Cesare Borgia
Willy Brandt
Leonid Brezhnev
Julius Caesar
John Calvin
Jimmy Carter
Fidel Castro
Catherine the Great
Charlemagne
Chiang Kai-Shek
Winston Churchill
Georges Clemenceau
Cleopatra
Constantine the Great
Hernán Cortés
Oliver Cromwell
Georges-Jacques
  Danton
Jefferson Davis
Moshe Dayan
Charles de Gaulle
Eamon De Valera
Eugene Debs
Deng Xiaoping
Benjamin Disraeli
Alexander Dubček
François & Jean-Claude
  Duvalier
Dwight Eisenhower
Eleanor of Aquitaine
Elizabeth I
Faisal
Ferdinand & Isabella
Francisco Franco
Benjamin Franklin

Frederick the Great
Indira Gandhi
Mohandas Gandhi
Giuseppe Garibaldi
Amin & Bashir Gemayel
Genghis Khan
William Gladstone
Mikhail Gorbachev
Ulysses S. Grant
Ernesto "Che" Guevara
Tenzin Gyatso
Alexander Hamilton
Dag Hammarskjöld
Henry VIII
Henry of Navarre
Paul von Hindenburg
Hirohito
Adolf Hitler
Ho Chi Minh
King Hussein
Ivan the Terrible
Andrew Jackson
James I
Wojciech Jaruzelski
Thomas Jefferson
Joan of Arc
Pope John XXIII
Pope John Paul II
Lyndon Johnson
Benito Juárez
John Kennedy
Robert Kennedy
Jomo Kenyatta
Ayatollah Khomeini
Nikita Khrushchev
Kim Il Sung
Martin Luther King, Jr.
Henry Kissinger
Kublai Khan
Lafayette
Robert E. Lee
Vladimir Lenin
Abraham Lincoln
David Lloyd George
Louis XIV
Martin Luther
Judas Maccabeus
James Madison
Nelson & Winnie
  Mandela
Mao Zedong
Ferdinand Marcos
George Marshall

Mary, Queen of Scots
Tomáš Masaryk
Golda Meir
Klemens von Metternich
James Monroe
Hosni Mubarak
Robert Mugabe
Benito Mussolini
Napoléon Bonaparte
Gamal Abdel Nasser
Jawaharlal Nehru
Nero
Nicholas II
Richard Nixon
Kwame Nkrumah
Daniel Ortega
Mohammed Reza Pahlavi
Thomas Paine
Charles Stewart
  Parnell
Pericles
Juan Perón
Peter the Great
Pol Pot
Muammar el-Qaddafi
Ronald Reagan
Cardinal Richelieu
Maximilien Robespierre
Eleanor Roosevelt
Franklin Roosevelt
Theodore Roosevelt
Anwar Sadat
Haile Selassie
Prince Sihanouk
Jan Smuts
Joseph Stalin
Sukarno
Sun Yat-sen
Tamerlane
Mother Teresa
Margaret Thatcher
Josip Broz Tito
Toussaint L'Ouverture
Leon Trotsky
Pierre Trudeau
Harry Truman
Queen Victoria
Lech Walesa
George Washington
Chaim Weizmann
Woodrow Wilson
Xerxes
Emiliano Zapata
Zhou Enlai

CHELSEA HOUSE PUBLISHERS

ON LEADERSHIP

Arthur M. Schlesinger, jr.

LEADERSHIP, it may be said, is really what makes the world go round. Love no doubt smooths the passage; but love is a private transaction between consenting adults. Leadership is a public transaction with history. The idea of leadership affirms the capacity of individuals to move, inspire, and mobilize masses of people so that they act together in pursuit of an end. Sometimes leadership serves good purposes, sometimes bad; but whether the end is benign or evil, great leaders are those men and women who leave their personal stamp on history.

Now, the very concept of leadership implies the proposition that individuals can make a difference. This proposition has never been universally accepted. From classical times to the present day, eminent thinkers have regarded individuals as no more than the agents and pawns of larger forces, whether the gods and goddesses of the ancient world or, in the modern era, race, class, nation, the dialectic, the will of the people, the spirit of the times, history itself. Against such forces, the individual dwindles into insignificance.

So contends the thesis of historical determinism. Tolstoy's great novel *War and Peace* offers a famous statement of the case. Why, Tolstoy asked, did millions of men in the Napoleonic Wars, denying their human feelings and their common sense, move back and forth across Europe slaughtering their fellows? "The war," Tolstoy answered, "was bound to happen simply because it was bound to happen." All prior history predetermined it. As for leaders, they, Tolstoy said, "are but the labels that serve to give a name to an end and, like labels, they have the least possible connection with the event." The greater the leader, "the more conspicuous the inevitability and the predestination of every act he commits." The leader, said Tolstoy, is "the slave of history."

Determinism takes many forms. Marxism is the determinism of class. Nazism the determinism of race. But the idea of men and women as the slaves of history runs athwart the deepest human instincts. Rigid determinism abolishes the idea of human freedom—

the assumption of free choice that underlies every move we make, every word we speak, every thought we think. It abolishes the idea of human responsibility, since it is manifestly unfair to reward or punish people for actions that are by definition beyond their control. No one can live consistently by any deterministic creed. The Marxist states prove this themselves by their extreme susceptibility to the cult of leadership.

More than that, history refutes the idea that individuals make no difference. In December 1931 a British politician crossing Park Avenue in New York City between 76th and 77th Streets around 10:30 P.M. looked in the wrong direction and was knocked down by an automobile—a moment, he later recalled, of a man aghast, a world aglare: "I do not understand why I was not broken like an eggshell or squashed like a gooseberry." Fourteen months later an American politician, sitting in an open car in Miami, Florida, was fired on by an assassin; the man beside him was hit. Those who believe that individuals make no difference to history might well ponder whether the next two decades would have been the same had Mario Constasino's car killed Winston Churchill in 1931 and Giuseppe Zangara's bullet killed Franklin Roosevelt in 1933. Suppose, in addition, that Adolf Hitler had been killed in the street fighting during the Munich *Putsch* of 1923 and that Lenin had died of typhus during World War I. What would the 20th century be like now?

For better or for worse, individuals do make a difference. "The notion that a people can run itself and its affairs anonymously," wrote the philosopher William James, "is now well known to be the silliest of absurdities. Mankind does nothing save through initiatives on the part of inventors, great or small, and imitation by the rest of us—these are the sole factors in human progress. Individuals of genius show the way, and set the patterns, which common people then adopt and follow."

Leadership, James suggests, means leadership in thought as well as in action. In the long run, leaders in thought may well make the greater difference to the world. But, as Woodrow Wilson once said, "Those only are leaders of men, in the general eye, who lead in action. . . . It is at their hands that new thought gets its translation into the crude language of deeds." Leaders in thought often invent in solitude and obscurity, leaving to later generations the tasks of imitation. Leaders in action—the leaders portrayed in this series—have to be effective in their own time.

And they cannot be effective by themselves. They must act in response to the rhythms of their age. Their genius must be adapted, in a phrase of William James's, "to the receptivities of the moment." Leaders are useless without followers. "There goes the mob," said the French politician hearing a clamor in the streets. "I am their leader. I must follow them." Great leaders turn the inchoate emotions of the mob to purposes of their own. They seize on the opportunities of their time, the hopes, fears, frustrations, crises, potentialities. They succeed when events have prepared the way for them, when the community is awaiting to be aroused, when they can provide the clarifying and organizing ideas. Leadership ignites the circuit between the individual and the mass and thereby alters history.

It may alter history for better or for worse. Leaders have been responsible for the most extravagant follies and most monstrous crimes that have beset suffering humanity. They have also been vital in such gains as humanity has made in individual freedom, religious and racial tolerance, social justice, and respect for human rights.

There is no sure way to tell in advance who is going to lead for good and who for evil. But a glance at the gallery of men and women in *World Leaders—Past and Present* suggests some useful tests.

One test is this: Do leaders lead by force or by persuasion? By command or by consent? Through most of history leadership was exercised by the divine right of authority. The duty of followers was to defer and to obey. "Theirs not to reason why / Theirs but to do and die." On occasion, as with the so-called enlightened despots of the 18th century in Europe, absolutist leadership was animated by humane purposes. More often, absolutism nourished the passion for domination, land, gold, and conquest and resulted in tyranny.

The great revolution of modern times has been the revolution of equality. The idea that all people should be equal in their legal condition has undermined the old structure of authority, hierarchy, and deference. The revolution of equality has had two contrary effects on the nature of leadership. For equality, as Alexis de Tocqueville pointed out in his great study *Democracy in America*, might mean equality in servitude as well as equality in freedom.

"I know of only two methods of establishing equality in the political world," Tocqueville wrote. "Rights must be given to every citizen, or none at all to anyone . . . save one, who is the master of all." There was no middle ground "between the sovereignty of all and the absolute power of one man." In his astonishing prediction

9

of 20th-century totalitarian dictatorship, Tocqueville explained how the revolution of equality could lead to the *"Führerprinzip"* and more terrible absolutism than the world had ever known.

But when rights are given to every citizen and the sovereignty of all is established, the problem of leadership takes a new form, becomes more exacting than ever before. It is easy to issue commands and enforce them by the rope and the stake, the concentration camp and the *gulag.* It is much harder to use argument and achievement to overcome opposition and win consent. The Founding Fathers of the United States understood the difficulty. They believed that history had given them the opportunity to decide, as Alexander Hamilton wrote in the first Federalist Paper, whether men are indeed capable of basing government on "reflection and choice, or whether they are forever destined to depend . . . on accident and force."

Government by reflection and choice called for a new style of leadership and a new quality of followership. It required leaders to be responsive to popular concerns, and it required followers to be active and informed participants in the process. Democracy does not eliminate emotion from politics; sometimes it fosters demagoguery; but it is confident that, as the greatest of democratic leaders put it, you cannot fool all of the people all of the time. It measures leadership by results and retires those who overreach or falter or fail.

It is true that in the long run despots are measured by results too. But they can postpone the day of judgment, sometimes indefinitely, and in the meantime they can do infinite harm. It is also true that democracy is no guarantee of virtue and intelligence in government, for the voice of the people is not necessarily the voice of God. But democracy, by assuring the right of opposition, offers built-in resistance to the evils inherent in absolutism. As the theologian Reinhold Niebuhr summed it up, "Man's capacity for justice makes democracy possible, but man's inclination to injustice makes democracy necessary."

A second test for leadership is the end for which power is sought. When leaders have as their goal the supremacy of a master race or the promotion of totalitarian revolution or the acquisition and exploitation of colonies or the protection of greed and privilege or the preservation of personal power, it is likely that their leadership will do little to advance the cause of humanity. When their goal is the abolition of slavery, the liberation of women, the enlargement of opportunity for the poor and powerless, the extension of equal rights to racial minorities, the defense of the freedoms of expression and opposition, it is likely that their leadership will increase the sum of human liberty and welfare.

Leaders have done great harm to the world. They have also conferred great benefits. You will find both sorts in this series. Even "good" leaders must be regarded with a certain wariness. Leaders are not demigods; they put on their trousers one leg after another just like ordinary mortals. No leader is infallible, and every leader needs to be reminded of this at regular intervals. Irreverence irritates leaders but is their salvation. Unquestioning submission corrupts leaders and demeans followers. Making a cult of a leader is always a mistake. Fortunately hero worship generates its own antidote. "Every hero," said Emerson, "becomes a bore at last."

The signal benefit the great leaders confer is to embolden the rest of us to live according to our own best selves, to be active, insistent, and resolute in affirming our own sense of things. For great leaders attest to the reality of human freedom against the supposed inevitabilities of history. And they attest to the wisdom and power that may lie within the most unlikely of us, which is why Abraham Lincoln remains the supreme example of great leadership. A great leader, said Emerson, exhibits new possibilities to all humanity. "We feed on genius. . . . Great men exist that there may be greater men."

Great leaders, in short, justify themselves by emancipating and empowering their followers. So humanity struggles to master its destiny, remembering with Alexis de Tocqueville: "It is true that around every man a fatal circle is traced beyond which he cannot pass; but within the wide verge of that circle he is powerful and free; as it is with man, so with communities."

1

An Enemy of the Wealthy

The summer of 1891 was one of the hottest ever recorded in Russia. Day after day, the skies stayed cloudless, rivers and creeks ran lower and lower, and the ground began to bake. Cattle grazed on yellowed grass and wasted away to skin and bones. The crops that had been planted in the spring began to wilt. The prospect of famine came closer and closer as the burning sky pressed down on the landscape like a sheet of white-hot metal.

Many of the peasants owned so little land that they rarely managed to do more than subsist even in years when the harvest was good. This situation had resulted from a major reform instituted three decades earlier. Before the reform, those who toiled in Russia's fields had been *serfs*, or slaves. As serfs, they were the legal private property of the landowning noblemen whose estates they worked. They were treated not as human beings, but classed alongside animals and equipment.

What was impressive about the young Lenin was the maturity of his thought, the balance of his intellectual forces, the sureness of his attack.
—LEON TROTSKY
leading Russian
revolutionary

Russian revolutionary Vladimir Ilich Ulyanov was arrested in 1896 by the secret police in St. Petersburg, the Russian capital, for spreading socialist propaganda among the city's workers. Ulyanov is known to history by the name that he adopted in 1899: Lenin.

In 1861 Alexander II, Russia's *tsar*, or emperor, gave the serfs — who at that time made up four-fifths of the country's total population of 80 million — their freedom. Russia's million-strong army, the ranks of which included more than 900,000 serfs, had recently been beaten in a war with Britain and France, and when the tsar learned of the unrest that had swept the countryside after the conflict, he decided that he could only retain the loyalty of the army by abolishing serfdom.

The newly freed serfs soon discovered that they had merely exchanged personal servitude for financial enslavement. The government allowed the nobles to keep most of their land, thus providing the peasants with woefully inadequate plots, and imposed crippling taxes and mortgages on the peasants to raise money with which to compensate their former owners. As a result, the peasants, who had anticipated receiving outright grants of land, came to feel a violent hatred for their former masters and the government tax collectors that deepened with every passing year. In 1891, when one of the worst droughts in the country's history struck, bringing in its wake an equally terrible famine, the government of Alexander III, Alexander II's son and successor, would provide no relief. It was then that

A peasant woman works in a village in southern Russia's Samara region. In 1892 famine brought widespread starvation to Samara. Lenin, who was living there at the time, openly criticized the relief programs instituted by the local middle classes.

popular resentment of the government's indifference to the suffering of the common people shook the tsarist system to its core.

Although hundreds of thousands of peasants were starving, the government continued to export the grain that had been stockpiled from previous harvests or purchased from producers in parts of the country that had not been ravaged by drought. By the end of 1891, millions of desperate peasants had abandoned their villages to seek bread and employment in the cities. Many who set out on this grim journey never reached their destinations: The corpses of infants and the elderly littered the roadsides, left unburied where they had fallen because those who survived them had to save their strength for walking.

Russia's tsar Alexander III poses with his six children, one of whom (rear center) would succeed him as Tsar Nicholas II. Extremely conservative, Alexander refused to give Russia a constitution and canceled many of the liberal reforms instituted by his father, Tsar Alexander II.

The peasants' destitution was the price the government chose to pay for keeping up the rapid pace of Russia's industrialization. Russia was the least developed of the European powers at that time, and the government was determined to remedy the situation. In exchange for the grain it exported, Russia received the up-to-date equipment its manufacturers needed to compete in the world economy. That this emphasis on exports was costing innumerable lives was unimportant to the government.

The government, however, merely ruled the Russian people — it did not represent them. The country knew no laws other than those approved by the tsar, and those laws were enforced by the dreaded secret police. Unlike many of its western European neighbors, Russia had never known democracy. Those members of its wealthier, educated classes — especially the *intelligentsia*, or radical intellectuals — who did not support the government saw the introduction of democracy as a vital first step toward preventing the instability that can plague a country whose political progress lags behind its economic progress.

Peasant women walk the streets of Moscow in search of work during Russia's pre-revolutionary period. During the famine that swept Russia in 1891–92, millions of desperate peasants abandoned their villages to seek employment in the cities.

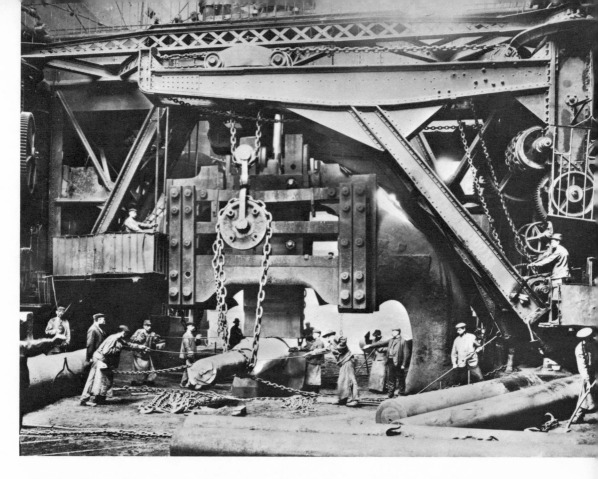

As the famine developed, the authorities at first attempted to play the situation down, suggesting that there had merely been a poor harvest. In many parts of Russia, however, thousands of middle-class people, confronted with endless columns of sick and starving peasants converging on every town and city, financed relief programs with their own money, setting up soup kitchens and arranging free medical treatment. Many government officials considered this demonstration of compassion for the poor subversive, suspecting that some of those engaging in philanthropy were thereby expressing their dissatisfaction with the regime.

What the government did not know was that its most dangerous enemies were as hostile toward those who helped the peasants as they were toward tsarism. And it was at the height of the famine that a young Russian named Vladimir Ilich Ulyanov, who is known to history as Lenin, emerged as the leading engineer of the destruction of the tsarist order.

Workers tend a forging hammer at a German metallurgical factory in 1861. Throughout the late 19th century, in an effort to accelerate Russia's industrialization, the tsarist government exchanged grain for such machinery, even when poor harvests left millions of peasants starving.

Hungry Russian peasants are fed at a soup kitchen set up by middle-class philanthropists in 1892. Lenin contended that the middle classes were aiding the destitute only to prevent social disturbances.

At the beginning of 1892, Ulyanov, a 21-year-old lawyer, was living in Samara, a small city in southern Russia's Volga River region. He knew that many middle-class Samarans were organizing relief services for the peasants, but he refused to participate in their activities himself. Ulyanov had, in fact, astonished many of his acquaintances by condemning the relief programs. Such programs, he believed, would only hold the country back.

Ulyanov's seemingly callous attitude had its basis in his political convictions. The young lawyer was an avid student of the work of Karl Marx, the 19th-century German economic, social, and political philosopher whose writings form the basis of modern communist thought. Marx believed that capitalism — the economic system based on private enterprise — contains the seeds of its own destruction, and that it must eventually be replaced by communism, a socioeconomic order in which private property has been abolished and people live without classes or other social divisions. According to the radical thinkers who built upon the foundation that Marx

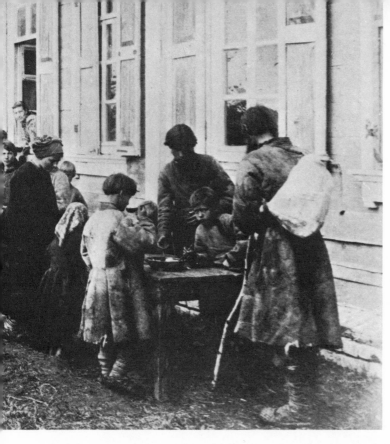

had laid, communism can only be realized following the creation of an intermediate order called socialism, in which the *proletariat*, or urban industrial working class, owns the means of production — the land and the factories.

Marx also held that the transition from capitalism to socialism can only be achieved by revolution, that control of the means of production must be seized by the proletariat from the *bourgeoisie* — the social class defined by Marx's colleague Friedrich Engels as "the class of modern capitalists, owners of the means of social production and employers of wage labor" — because no bourgeois will give up his property willingly in the interests of progress toward socialism. Another important element of Marx's teachings was his contention that worldwide communism is historically inevitable because both class war between capitalists and workers *and* the workers' victory over the capitalists are historically inevitable.

All these ideas were firmly implanted in young Ulyanov's mind when he attacked Samara's middle

The work of Karl Marx, the 19th-century German economist and political philosopher, forms the basis of modern communist thought. Lenin first read *Das Kapital*, (*Capital*), Marx's masterpiece, in 1888.

class in 1892. There was another belief, however, that lay at the heart of his argument. According to Marx, only a politicized proletariat can achieve its own emancipation: The workers cannot begin their march toward freedom and equality until they know that they have the power to advance their own interests, until they understand the reasons why they live and work in bad conditions. And, again according to Marx, the proletariat becomes politicized faster than the peasantry because it has more awareness of its own potential than the peasantry: Workers in the cities have more access to the world of ideas — to newspapers, books, and journals — than their rural counterparts, and as they organize into unions to protect their interests, they develop their own political culture and gain a deeper understanding of their situation.

Ulyanov, like most Marxists at that time, saw the expansion of the proletariat as a vital part of the process that leads to the destruction of capitalism: As capitalism expanded, so too would the class that was destined to destroy it. And that is why he viewed the middle class's efforts to help the peasants as a threat to the kind of progress he wanted to see in Russia. The more peasants famine forced into the cities, the faster the proletariat would grow. As Russian radical writer V. Vodovozov recounts in his *My Acquaintance with Lenin*, Ulyanov asserted: "The famine is the direct consequence of a particular social order. So long as that order exists, famines are inevitable. They can be abolished only by the abolition of that order of society. Being in this sense inevitable, famine today performs a progressive function. It destroys the peasant economy and throws peasants from the village into the city. . . . It will cause the peasant to reflect on the fundamental facts of capitalist society. It will destroy his faith in the Tsar and in Tsarism and will in time speed the victory of the revolution." The fact that Ulyanov belonged to the class he was attacking made his words seem all the more provocative: "The famine threatens to create serious disturbances and possibly the destruction of the entire bourgeois order."

Twenty-six years later Ulyanov would make yet another analysis of a critical situation that stunned all who heard it. On that occasion, however, the audience would be largely composed of his fellow revolutionaries, and Russia would be in turmoil, on the verge of total defeat in war and lacking an effective government. On April 17, 1917, Ulyanov would offer his colleagues a prescription for ending the confusion to the advantage of socialism, a prescription that seemed to contradict almost everything he had said to date on the subject of how best to break the bourgeoisie and turn Russia into a workers' state. And six months later, having converted his colleagues to his own vision of the future, he would mastermind one of the most momentous events in 20th-century history, an event with which he will always be identified—the Russian Revolution of 1917.

This is the story of Lenin, architect of revolution, founding father of the Union of Soviet Socialist Republics, and Marx's most influential intellectual disciple.

[Marx] shared the individualist radicalism of his time. He . . . assumed that it was highly desirable to strangle the last king with the bowels of the last priest; and he believed that inestimable benefit would follow from this. His only novelty was to show that the last capitalists . . . should be strangled at the same time.
—A. J. P. TAYLOR
British historian

2

The Nobleman's Son

Vladimir Ilich Ulyanov was born in Simbirsk, a city in southern Russia, on April 22, 1870. He was the third child and second son of Ilya Nikolayevich Ulyanov, who was one of Simbirsk's most respected citizens, and Maria Aleksandrovna Ulyanova. Ilya Nikolayevich held the prestigious position of inspector of public schools for the administrative district of Simbirsk. He greatly enjoyed his work, especially because it brought him into contact with the children of the peasants. A man with a social conscience, Ilya Nikolayevich wanted to do as much as he could to help free the peasants from ignorance and superstition. In 1874, when Vladimir was four years old, Ilya Nikolayevich was promoted director of public schools for Simbirsk, a position that brought with it elevation to the status of *chinovnik*, or member of the hereditary nobility and lifetime servant of the state.

Facts are stubborn things.
—LENIN

Lenin's parents, Maria Alexasndrovna Ulyanova and Ilya Nikolayevich Ulyanov, pose with their children at the family home in Simbirsk in 1879. Standing (left to right) are Olga, Aleksandr, and Anna; sitting are Maria, Dmitry, and Vladimir.

Four-year-old Lenin with his younger sister Olga in 1874. One year later, Lenin's mother took charge of her son's early schooling, teaching him to read and to play the piano.

Vladimir received his earliest education from his mother, who taught him to read and to play the piano. In 1879 he entered the Simbirsk *gymnasium*, or classical school. During the eight years he spent there Vladimir was usually at the head of his class, showing at an early age the immense capacity for systematic work that would distinguish him throughout his life.

Whenever he was not at school or busy with his homework, Vladimir would go for long walks in the countryside, read, or play chess with his older brother, Aleksandr. Four years Vladimir's senior, Aleksandr was a quiet, single-minded, and intelligent young man: Vladimir adored him. In 1886, when his father died at age 55, Aleksandr, who by then was studying biology at the university in St. Petersburg, the Russian capital, became the head of the family.

Ilya Nikolayevich's death came as a terrible blow to Vladimir. Then, fourteen months later, tragedy struck again. In March 1887 the police in St. Petersburg discovered that a group of dissident students were plotting to assassinate Alexander III: Aleksandr Ulyanov was one of the students arrested in the roundup that followed. He had been using his extensive knowledge of chemistry to manufacture bombs intended to mete out to Alexander III the same fate that Alexander II had suffered in 1881. The police also arrested Aleksandr's sister Anna, who was also studying in St. Petersburg at that time.

Nikolay Gavrilovich Chernyshevsky, the 19th-century Russian economist and author, profoundly influenced Ulyanov and thousands of other Russian left-wing dissidents. Lenin borrowed the title of a Chernyshevsky novel, *What Is To Be Done?*, for one of his own tracts.

Lenin idolized his older brother, Aleksandr, who was the leader of a left-wing terrorist group. Aleksandr was executed on May 20, 1887, for plotting to kill Tsar Alexander III, and his death planted the idea of revenge in the mind of his younger brother.

None of Aleksandr's relatives, including Vladimir, had ever suspected that he had revolutionary inclinations. Now it was revealed that he had been the leader of a terrorist group modeled on the one that had killed Alexander II: the People's Will. As a member of this organization, Aleksandr was part of a tradition of revolutionary opposition to the tsarist autocracy that had its basis in the various ideologies of the radical intellectual movement known as Populism.

The Populists were Russia's first revolutionary socialists. The two great figures of early Populism were Aleksandr Herzen, who published an influential journal called *The Bell* while living in exile in western Europe during the 1850s and 1860s, and an economist named Nikolay Gavrilovich Chernyshevsky, whose work Marx greatly admired.

In 1862 the first Populist underground movement, Land and Freedom, was formed. Its members took their inspiration from two leading Populist theorists, Mikhail Bakunin and Pyotr Lavrovich Lavrov. Bakunin, an anarchist, believed that the peasants were ready to rise up against the tsarist state and replace it with cooperative institutions, or collectives. Lavrov wanted the Populists to concentrate on spreading socialist ideas among the peasants. His method, he believed, would eventually result in the creation of a class of revolutionary leaders drawn from within the peasantry.

Land and Freedom's first expedition to the countryside was also its last. In the summer of 1874, thousands of dissident students descended upon Russia's rural areas, intending to live among the peasants while trying to persuade them to embrace socialism and revolt against the tsar. The vast majority of the peasants proved unreceptive to the students' ideas, however. They were extremely conservative, idolized the tsar, and did not like being told that they were in need of "enlightenment." By the end of the year, most of the students had been betrayed to the police by the very people they had hoped to convert.

Having concluded that the peasants were not a revolutionary class, Land and Freedom revised its philosophy and tactics. The principle theorist to whose ideas they turned was Pyotr Tkachev. Tkachev believed that in Russia socialism would have to be imposed not from below, by politicized peasants, but from above, by a revolutionary group that, having seized power, would use the administrative machinery of the state to carry out socialist reforms. Tkachev's ideas would eventually influence a generation of Russian Marxist revolutionaries, including Ulyanov.

In 1879 debate about the role of terrorism split Land and Freedom into two irreconcilable factions: the People's Will, whose members viewed terrorism against government officials and the tsar as the only means of waking up the populace, and the Black Repartition, which rejected terrorism and advocated the redistribution of the land among the "Black Folk," as the peasants were known. The Black Repartition's principals were the first leading Russian revolutionaries to condemn the idea of peasant-based socialism as utopian and follow the traditional Marxist tenet that the proletariat is the real revolutionary class. The movement's leading theorists were Vera Zasulich, Paul Akselrod, and Georgy Valentinovich Plekhanov.

Despite the police persecution that followed the assassination of Alexander II, many young radicals attempted to resurrect the People's Will. And Aleksandr Ulyanov was one of them.

On May 20, 1887, Aleksandr and four of his co-conspirators were executed in St. Petersburg. Aleksandr's sister Anna, against whom the authorities had found no hard evidence of involvement in the plot, was exiled to Kokushkino, an estate that Maria Aleksandrovna had inherited from her father, and placed under police surveillance.

Vladimir's inexpressive reaction to the news of his brother's death surprised nobody. While at the *gymnasium*, from which he was about to graduate, he had gained a considerable reputation for reserve.

In 1897 tsarist authorities sentenced Lenin to a three-year term of exile in the remote Russian province of Siberia. At that time, he was waging a bitter ideological battle against the "Legal Marxists," whose belief that socialism could be achieved without recourse to violent revolution he thought utterly unrealistic.

Known as "the father of Russian Marxism," Russian Social Democrat Georgy Valentinovich Plekhanov, whose work greatly influenced Lenin, believed in the revolutionary potential of the proletariat. In 1883 he founded the Group for the Emancipation of Labor.

He simply said: "I'll make them pay for this! I swear it!"

Following his graduation in June 1887, Vladimir applied for admission to Kazan University, where he wanted to study law. At this point in his life, he still believed that Russia could only be changed by legal means, not by revolutionary action.

Although Ulyanov gained excellent marks in his entrance examinations, he realized that the university authorities might not look kindly on the brother of an executed terrorist. He gained admission, nonetheless, with the assistance of the director of the *gymnasium*, Fyodor Kerensky, who wrote a glowing testimonial for him. In August 1887, Maria Aleksandrovna sold the house in Simbirsk, and the whole family moved to Kazan.

Ulyanov's undergraduate career at Kazan University ended just weeks after it began. In December 1887 he went to a student meeting held to protest the government's decision to close down fraternity clubs on the ground that they were hotbeds of sedition. Police spies noted the names of the students who attended, and Ulyanov, even though he had done nothing wrong, was expelled from the university.

Ulyanov spent the next nine months under police surveillance, living with Anna at Kokushkino. Maria Aleksandrovna joined them there. She wrote hundreds of letters to family friends in government service in St. Petersburg, begging them to use their influence to secure her children's release from official supervision. In the summer of 1888, the authorities allowed Ulyanov and Anna to return to Kazan. Ulyanov was not, however, allowed to resume his studies, and his request for permission to study abroad was denied.

During the fall of 1888, Ulyanov became familiar with the work of Karl Marx. He was loaned a copy of the first volume of the German philosopher's masterpiece, *Das Kapital* (*Capital*), by the members of a local Social Democratic study circle. (At this time, most Marxists called themselves Social Democrats.) In *Das Kapital*, Marx analyzes the principles that

Tsar Nicholas II, seen here with his wife, Tsarina Alexandra, was an indecisive ruler who failed to understand the social tensions in Russia during his reign. Their political ineptitude damaged the prestige of the Romanov dynasty in the eyes of many Russians.

govern the development of capitalism and develops his theory of historical materialism, which holds that the labor process itself is the prime influence on the development of human history and that the workers, who make the production process happen, actually *make* history in so doing.

Das Kapital electrified Ulyanov. Here, at last, he felt, was a philosophy that explained the modern world, that demonstrated the inevitability of socialism and anticipated the creation of a new order of society in which men and women, instead of being slaves of their employers and spending their lives working at degrading jobs for subsistence wages, would manage their own affairs and lead happy and creative existences.

While he read Marx, Ulyanov also studied the work of Plekhanov, who was now living in exile in Switzerland and, together with Akselrod and Zasulich, had founded an organization called the Groups for the Emancipation of Labor. Plekhanov's contention that the Russian revolution would come in two stages—first, a revolution against the tsarist system to establish democracy and speed up the development of capitalism, and then the socialist revolution as a natural result of the development and eventual self-destruction of capitalism — greatly appealed to Ulyanov. Consequently, by the end of 1890, when he received permission to take his law examinations in St. Petersburg, he had gained a deep understanding of Marx's work and of the work of Marx's most important Russian disciple.

Under the terms of the conditions imposed on him by the university authorities, Ulyanov prepared for his law examinations as an "external student." This meant that, instead of attending lectures and seminars like a regular student, he had to teach himself from books. The authorities did not want him to mix with the other students. Despite this seemingly overwhelming disadvantage, Ulyanov finished the required reading for the standard four-year law course in just 12 months and, in November 1891, passed his examinations with great distinction, coming out at the top of his class.

> *The Revolutionist is a doomed man. . . . His entire being is devoured by one purpose, one thought, one passion— the revolution.*
>
> —MIKHAIL BAKUNIN and
> SERGEY NECHAYEV
> 19th-century anarchists

Leading 19th-century Russian novelist Leo Tolstoy (left), an outspoken advocate of social reform in Russia, converses with Maxim Gorky, a prominent Russian author who became one of Lenin's closest political allies.

During the year that he spent studying for his examinations, Ulyanov furthered his education as a socialist, translating Marx and Engels's *The Communist Manifesto* into Russian from the original German. In this important tract, Marx and Engels portray history as a succession of class struggles, assert that the proletariat must be the instrument of its own emancipation, and state that "Communists everywhere . . . openly declare that their ends can be attained only by the forcible overthrow of all existing social conditions."

Having gained his degree, Vladimir worked as a lawyer in Samara. Within two years, however, he admitted to himself that he was only pursuing a respectable career in a provincial town because that was what his mother — who feared that his Marxist inclinations would lead him down the same path Alexandr had traveled — wanted him to do. In 1893 Ulyanov set out for St. Petersburg to begin his true life's work.

3

Social Democracy and Its Discontents

In St. Petersburg, Ulyanov quickly emerged as a Social Democrat who kept theory and practice closely interconnected. Considering progress possible only when the workers were familiar with socialist ideas and the revolutionaries fully acquainted with the situation and attitudes of the proletariat, Ulyanov spent much of his time visiting the city's poorest districts to ask people about the conditions in which they lived and worked. Because police spies were always keeping track of dissidents, Ulyanov traveled to the working-class districts in disguise, taking roundabout routes and doubling back repeatedly to make sure he was not being followed.

Within a few months, Ulyanov gained recognition as the leading theorist of the influential St. Petersburg Social Democratic group known as the "Elders." By the end of 1894, he had managed to persuade the organization's more radical members to abandon their previous policy of discouraging the select groups of workers to whom they taught Marxist theory from taking part in strikes and other types of industrial action.

> *The principal idea of [Lenin] as we understood it was that the working class did not yet know how to make use of its potentialities.*
> —VLADIMIR KNIAZEV
> Russian dockworker

Lenin in March 1897, shortly before his deportation from St. Petersburg to Siberia. During his last year of internal exile, 1899, Lenin penned *Aims of the Russian Social Democrats*, the first tract he wrote under the pseudonym Lenin.

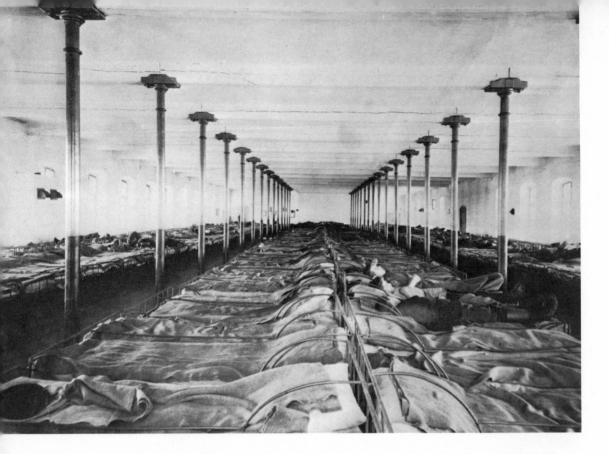

The workers' dormitory at St. Petersburg's Ivanov factory is one of thousands of buildings that housed Russia's proletarians during the prerevolutionary era. Between 1893 and 1895, Lenin interviewed numerous St. Petersburg workers at their homes and in factory dormitories to compile information on their living and working conditions.

Under Ulyanov's direction, each workers' study circle comprised a "cell" of six workers, who acted as a committee for direct agitation in the factories where they were employed. All the "cells" were kept separate from one another. They did not act collectively, and only Ulyanov knew them all. Messages were either written in invisible ink or coded. Illegal literature was printed up on secret presses and mimeographic machines.

To preclude the possibility of the entire network collapsing in the event that he was arrested, Ulyanov designated Nadezhda Konstaninovna Krupskaya, who was one of the few members of the Elders whom the police never followed, as his "successor." (Krupskaya, whom Ulyanov had first met at a meeting in the spring of 1894, was now one of his most trusted aides; she was also very much in love with him, and he with her.) Slowly but surely, Ulyanov succeeded in transforming the Elders from a glorified debating society into a highly structured, centrally directed revolutionary underground organization with effective links to St. Petersburg's proletariat — the raw material of socialist revolution.

During this period, Ulyanov's championing of the proletariat as the primary agent of revolution brought him into conflict not only with Populists, whose peasant-oriented socialism he rejected, but with those Social Democrats who did not regard Marxism as an ideology with which to mobilize the proletariat. One Social Democrat with whom Ulyanov clashed on this subject was Pyotr Struve, whose *Critical Notes on the Economic Development of Russia* became legally available in Russia in 1894, when the authorities began to relax their censorship of Marxist literature. (The government had decided that the revolutionary implications of much Marxist writing were effectively obscured by its highly technical nature, and that the Marxists' opposition to Populism — the movement the authorities *really* feared — should receive a measure of official encouragement.) Ulyanov's reaction to Struve's brand of Marxism, which envisaged a gradual transition from capitalism to socialism through a series of liberal reforms, was uncompromisingly hostile. "Legal Marxism," as the work of Struve and his intellectual disciples became known, seemed to Ulyanov as bourgeois as its authors.

During the fall of 1895, Ulyanov stepped up his revolutionary activities. Strikes had broken out in the factories, and Ulyanov spent much of his time writing revolutionary pamphlets and arranging for their distribution to the workers. Then, on December 20, disaster struck. The police, acting on information provided by an informant, pounced on the revolutionaries. Ulyanov and most of his senior lieutenants were arrested and thrown into jail.

Because the prison regulations were not particularly strict, captivity did not prevent Ulyanov from continuing to direct his organization's activities. The prison authorities allowed visitors twice a week, and Ulyanov's cell was soon piled high with books brought in by his sister Anna, who had written messages in them in a special code that Ulyanov had taught her. Using Anna and other members of the organization whom the police did not suspect of involvement with the revolutionary movement as go-betweens, Ulyanov maintained effective contact with his comrades outside.

St. Petersburg Social Democrat Nadezhda Konstaninovna Krupskaya, a dedicated dissident and brilliant political organizer, first met Lenin in 1894. She joined him in exile in 1898, following her own arrest by the tsarist police, and the two young revolutionaries were married that same year.

Lenin poses in 1896 with his senior lieutenants, some of whom had founded the League of Struggle for the Emancipation of Labor. Shortly after this photograph was taken, Lenin and one of his closest colleagues, Yulii Martov (seated, far right), were both arrested and imprisoned.

During his imprisonment, Ulyanov continued his rigorous work schedule. Using milk as invisible ink and molding lumps of bread as inkwells, he wrote numerous pamphlets that were then smuggled out and mimeographed. He also began researching and drafting his first full-length book, *The Development of Capitalism in Russia*, which was eventually published in 1899.

In February 1897 the authorities sentenced Ulyanov to a three-year term of internal exile under police surveillance in the eastern Russian province of Siberia. He arrived in the remote village of Shushenskoe in May, and rented a room in a house belonging to a well-to-do peasant. He had been permitted to bring as many books as he wanted with him, and more books arrived from St. Petersburg every day in the mail. At first, he enjoyed his enforced leisure, but it was not long before he got back down to work. Once again, he wrote a constant stream of letters and articles characterized by hatred for the bourgeoisie and devotion to the proletariat. His insistence on the revolutionary importance of the proletariat began to acquire a new intensity.

In March 1898, while Ulyanov was still in Siberia, Russian social democracy came closer to institutionalization as a political party. Six Russian Social Democrats and three members of the recently founded Jewish Workers' Alliance held a congress in Minsk, a city in western Russia. (The Jewish Workers' Alliance, which was commonly known as the Bund and representing mainly factory workers and craftsmen, was based in Lithuania, a Russian satellite state on the Baltic Sea, and in the section of Poland that Russia had occupied since 1815.) During the congress the two groups proclaimed the birth of the Russian Social Democratic Workers' party (RSDWP), established a central committee, and decided that the party should publish its own newspaper.

The delegates to the founding congress of the RSDWP were arrested just weeks after it dispersed, and none of them were involved in the subsequent development of the party. The manifesto that Struve (who had not been present at the conference) wrote for the party gained recognition, however, as a landmark in the annals of Social Democratic thought. The manifesto endorsed the concept of revolution in two stages — first, the bourgeois-democratic revolution, then the proletarian-socialist revolution — and stressed the fact that because the Russian bourgeoisie lacked the strength to make its own revolution, the leadership role in the bourgeois-democratic revolution would be assumed by the proletariat.

In May 1898 Ulyanov was reunited with Krupskaya, who had been arrested in St. Petersburg and sentenced to internal exile in the *gubernia* of Ufa in northern Russia. She had contrived, however, to get herself transferred to Shushenskoe by describing herself as Ulyanov's fiancée and agreeing to an official stipulation that she would face deportation to Ufa unless she married Ulyanov as soon as she arrived in Shushenskoe. The fact that the circumstances under which Ulyanov and Krupskaya got married were dictated by officialdom did nothing to diminish the happiness the two young people derived from being together at last.

The last 12 months of Ulyanov's exile were among the most intellectually tumultuous of his entire career. He learned of new developments in socialist

An imprisoned dissident rests between work periods at a labor camp in Siberia, where Lenin lived under police surveillance from 1897 to 1900. The "crimes" committed by many exiles were often no worse than reading officially forbidden books or taking part in progressive political discussion groups.

Leading Russian Marxists Leon Deutch (left) and Pavel Akselrod (right) were leading members of the editorial board of *The Spark*, the Russian Social-Democratic newspaper, first published in 1900. Lenin was largely instrumental in creating the publication.

thought, both inside Russia and abroad. Ulyanov, who was now writing under the name Lenin, was disturbed by many of these developments because they broke from orthodox Marxism. In Russia, Struve was now calling for a revision of all Marxist economic theory. Ulyanov's fury knew no bounds: The legal Marxists, he believed, were stripping Marxism of its revolutionary content. Equally appalling to Ulyanov was that, according to his orthodox Marxist colleagues in European Russia, these new ideas were gaining acceptance among a majority of Russian and western European Social Democrats.

It was also during this period that Lenin found himself confronted with a major exposition of a new, nonrevolutionary trend in German Social Democratic thought. In March 1899 a book entitled *Evolutionary Socialism* had been published in Germany. Its author, Eduard Bernstein, was a leading member of the German Social Democratic party (SPD), which was then the largest and most influential of the European socialist parties affiliated with the broad socialist organization known as the Second International of Social Democratic Parties. (The First International, which Marx had led, existed between 1864 and 1876.)

In *Evolutionary Socialism*, Bernstein rejected the idea of forcible revolution, asserting that capitalism could be changed into socialism by a gradual process of reform. By increasing its parliamentary representation and thereby legislating the extension of its political and economic rights, the working class, Bernstein held, would "gradually transform the state in the direction of democracy."

Bernstein's brand of Marxism, which became known as "revisionism," appalled Lenin, who now grew determined to counter what he considered the intellectual slovenliness and organizational ineptitude of this new socialist movement. Together with two of his fellow exiles, Aleksandr Potresov and Yulii Martov, Lenin planned to establish an uncompromisingly orthodox Social Democratic newspaper. Their hope was to publish it abroad and smuggle editions into Russia by a network of secret agents.

Addressing theoretical problems and defining practical tasks, the newspaper would act as the organizational nucleus of the RSDWP, as the very foundation of a unified, centrally directed, nationwide revolutionary party that would be invulnerable to the police and resistant to all forms of nonrevolutionary Marxism.

When Lenin's term of exile ended in February 1900, he and Krupskaya agreed that he should go abroad immediately. Krupskaya would stay behind to serve out the rest of her sentence and join Lenin later. On July 29, 1900, Lenin left for Munich, Germany, where the new journal, *Iskra* (*The Spark*), was to have its editorial offices.

The first issue of *Iskra* appeared on December 24, 1900, and thousands of copies were distributed throughout Russia by Lenin's agents. Many articles that Lenin wrote for *Iskra* concerned party organization. During the winter of 1901–02, he consolidated his thoughts on this subject in a tract entitled *What Is To Be Done?* (a title he borrowed from Chernyshevsky), which contained many of the ideas on revolutionary politics and party organization that have become known as "Leninism." The core of Lenin's argument in *What Is To Be Done?* is that only a centrally directed revolutionary movement composed "chiefly of people professionally engaged in revolutionary activity" and led by "a stable organization of leaders which preserves continuity" can rescue the workers from the oppression of the bourgeoisie and convert them to socialism.

Shortly after the publication of *What Is To Be Done?*, in March 1902, *Iskra* relocated to London, England. There most of Lenin's mornings were spent writing books and articles in the reading room of the British Museum, where Marx himself, who lived in London from 1849 until his death in 1883, had researched *Das Kapital*. In the afternoons, Lenin attended editorial meetings. In the evenings, he devoted his time to correspondence and further study.

It was also while he was living in London, in October 1902, that Lenin first met Leon Trotsky, a charismatic, resourceful, and articulate young man

Yulii Martov, who contended that the RSDWP should be open to anyone who supported its program, was bitterly condemned by Lenin at the party's second congress in August 1903. Lenin wanted the party composed solely of dedicated revolutionaries who would submit to the discipline of a central leadership.

Leon Trotsky, a resourceful and articulate young revolutionary, first met Lenin in London in October 1902. Later he became one of Lenin's closest colleagues and a giant of the Russian revolutionary movement.

who would later become one of his closest colleagues and a giant of the Russian revolutionary movement in his own right. The 23-year-old Trotsky, a Jew whose real name was Lev Davidovich Bronstein, had recently escaped from exile in Siberia. Trotsky was a brilliant writer, and several of his articles had greatly impressed Lenin.

By the beginning of 1903 Lenin's demands for *Iskra* to take a harder political line had begun to alienate both his London colleagues and Plekhanov and Akselrod, who had stayed in Switzerland. In April 1903, the editorial board voted for relocating to Geneva. Lenin, who had always feared that Plekhanov would dominate the editorial board if it met in Geneva, was the only board member to vote against the relocation.

In July 1903 the RSDWP met for its second congress, in Brussels, the capital of Belgium. A few days later, harassment of the delegates by tsarist spies and the Brussels police became so severe that the members of the congress decided to continue the proceedings in London. And it was there that a major disagreement about the nature of the party split the congress.

Lenin, firmly convinced that overthrowing the tsarist system required a highly centralized, disciplined organization, wanted the party to be open only to active, uniquely dedicated revolutionaries. Martov, on the other hand, wanted the party to be open to anyone who supported its program. Like Lenin, Martov wanted a centralized party, but he believed it should be a broad party, composed of workers and intellectuals who would have a say in party policy.

When the matter was put to a vote, 23 delegates — including Plekhanov — supported Lenin's formulation, while 28 supported Martov's. Those who supported Lenin's view withdrew to an anteroom. Lenin then mapped out a strategy to persuade the delegates who supported Martov to change their minds.

Lenin went without sleep for several days, arguing his case around the clock. Then, just when it had begun to seem that he would not succeed, the five Bundist delegates, who had voted for Martov's proposal, left the congress. Lenin, scenting the possibility of victory now that his opponents had lost their majority, shrewdly proposed that *The Workers' Cause*, a revisionist newspaper that was *Iskra*'s main rival for ideological supremacy within the party, be dissolved and *Iskra* recognized as the sole body representing the Social Democratic émigrés. Martov, not realizing that Lenin had set a trap for him, naturally voted in favor of Lenin's motion. As a result, two supporters of *The Worker's Cause* who had backed Martov on the membership issue and hated to see him betray his own convictions stormed out of the congress, never to return. Lenin was ecstatic: His original minority of five had now been converted to a majority of two. He immediately designated his own bloc the *Bolshevik*, or majority, wing, and thus brought into being the hard-line faction within Russian Social Democracy with which the RSDWP — and the Russian Revolution — would eventually be exclusively identified. Those who opposed him became known as the *Menshevik*, or minority, wing.

Lenin then engineered majority acceptance of his motion to make the party central committee, which was based inside Russia, completely subordinate to the *Iskra* board. Next he ousted Potresov, Zasulich, and Akselrod from the *Iskra* editorial board, getting himself, Plekhanov, and Martov elected in their place. When a vote was held to elect a chairman to the newly instituted, thoroughly "Leninist" party council, the congress chose Plekhanov, but in a manner that demonstrated that they resented the fact that the father of Russian Marxism had allowed himself to be hijacked by Lenin: Twenty-two of the 44 delegates abstained from voting. Still, Lenin continued to refer to his bloc as the Bolsheviks, to claim that he spoke for the majority and was thus entitled to his original mandate.

Bolshevism, the narrow, sectarian, and inflexibly dogmatic Leninist variant of Russian Social Democracy became a fact of political life. A new, fanatically adversarial politics, one whose followers were utterly convinced that they were the only true socialists, was born.

4

The Straight and Narrow Path

By the time the Second Congress of the RSDWP ended, on August 23, 1903, the two factions into which Lenin's relentless revolutionism had split the party were barely capable of communicating with each other. Plekhanov indicated that, out of deference to Akselrod and Zasulich, he would no longer back Lenin. When Plekhanov then demanded the reinstatement of the original *Iskra* editorial board, Lenin, recognizing that this would result in a Menshevik takeover of the newspaper that he wanted to serve as the mainstay of the RSDWP's revolutionary wing, handed in his resignation.

For a while thereafter, Lenin was almost completely isolated, sustained only by Krupskaya's unwavering support. Critics of Lenin's insistence on the subordination of the entire party to the central committee now included Plekhanov and also Trotsky, who, in a 1904 pamphlet, characterized Lenin's view as one in which "a single 'dictator' substitutes himself for the central committee."

> *The ultracentralism advocated by Lenin is not something born of a positive creative spirit but of a negative sterile spirit of the watchman. His line of thought is cut to the control of party activity . . . to its narrowing . . . to the role of taskmaster.*
> —ROSA LUXEMBURG
> leading Social-Democrat

Russian troops dispose of the bodies of Japanese soldiers at Port Arthur, a Chinese seaport leased by the Russian government, during the 1904–05 Russo-Japanese War. The serious defeats incurred by Russia's armies during the conflict engendered massive popular discontent and seriously damaged the credibility of the tsarist government.

Russian workers eat at a communal canteen. During the Russo-Japanese war, deliveries of food to Russian cities became erratic as the military commandeered an ever-increasing proportion of the country's transportation resources. The resultant food shortages triggered strikes in many cities.

In response not only to his critics' charges that he had no regard for democracy but also, more importantly, in response to changing circumstances inside Russia, Lenin developed his theory of democratic centralism. A less rigid version of centralism, this theory allows for all party members to participate in devising policy and electing leaders. Once policy has been established, however, the party rank and file are responsible for its implementation and obliged to demonstrate absolute loyalty to the party leadership.

Still, Trotsky was convinced that Lenin's methods would lead not to the dictatorship of the proletariat — according to Marx, a form of regime in which the proletariat assumes the dominant position in society, governing itself — but, to a "dictatorship over the proletariat."

In the fall of 1904, Lenin met with a group of 22 Bolshevik émigrés and announced that *Forward*, a new Bolshevik journal that he planned to publish, would be "the real organ of the working-class movement in Russia." Lenin then persuaded his listeners to endorse his contention that the existing bodies of the RSDWP no longer represented the will of the majority of the party. The first issue of *Forward* appeared in December 1904. At about the same time, important developments inside Russia intruded upon the activities of Lenin and his colleagues, radically altering the context within which they were working.

Earlier that year, in February, the Japanese navy had staged a surprise attack on the Russian fleet's Far Eastern squadron at Port Arthur, thus launching the 1904–05 Russo-Japanese War, which was fought for colonies in Asia. By the end of 1904, Russia's armies had suffered several serious defeats, and public discontent had grown widespread. The war placed a tremendous strain on the country's transportation system, and deliveries of food to the cities became increasingly erratic and then broke down altogether. As bread prices soared, the workers faced starvation, and spontaneous strikes erupted in major cities.

On January 22, 1905, a liberal priest named Father George Gapon led 200,000 St. Petersburg workers on a peaceful march to Tsar Nicholas II's sumptuous Winter Palace to present a petition that called for an eight-hour workday and a guaranteed minimum wage. The tsar was absent from the city, however, and when the marchers entered the Winter Palace square, the commander of the troops that had been deployed to prevent them from reaching the palace, frightened by the size of the demonstration, panicked and ordered the soldiers to open fire. Within minutes, the deep snow in front of the Winter Palace was stained with the blood of hundreds of dying and wounded workers. The disaster triggered a general strike in St. Petersburg and other cities.

When the tsar returned, he initiated a campaign of repression. It soon became apparent, however, that the massacre had shattered what little faith the public still had in the regime, and the tsar found that he had no choice but to accept his advisers' recommendation that he declare himself willing to permit the creation of a consultative assembly, or *Duma*.

When Lenin heard about the violence at the Winter Palace he concluded that an armed insurrection and the establishment of a workers' and peasants' dictatorship were now feasible objectives. In April 1905 he and his followers gathered in London for a conference that Lenin termed the Third Congress of the RSDWP, despite the fact that it was attended only by Bolsheviks. The delegates endorsed Lenin as party leader, and supported his proposal that the party should prepare for an armed uprising. Lenin's supporters did not, however, accept his advocacy of democratic centralism, which Lenin promoted because he now believed that, as the impetus toward revolution increased, public life in Russia would become more open. The Bolsheviks, he felt, should now accept a revision of the hard-line centralist approach he had previously espoused — the philosophy that had attracted his present supporters in the first place — and permit greater autonomy for local party

Senior clergymen of the Russian Orthodox church, which was the country's established church during the pre-revolutionary era. In his 1905 pamphlet *Socialism and Religion*, Lenin, an atheist, argued for the separation of church and state.

This **Moscow fruit store shel-
tered a clandestine socialist
printing press throughout
1905. In December of that
year, tsarist troops moved
against the revolutionary
strongholds in Moscow's
working-class districts, kill-
ing more than 1,000 men,
women, and children in the
process.**

committees. Lenin's followers fought against the new proposals, but eventually conceded.

The situation to which Lenin wanted the Bolsheviks to adapt became increasingly volatile during the spring and summer of 1905. In June, the Russian battleship *Potemkin* steamed into harbor at the Black Sea port of Odessa flying the red flag — the traditional banner of the revolutionary movement. The *Potemkin*'s crew, tired of bad food and abysmal living conditions, had mutinied, shooting, throwing overboard, or imprisoning all the ship's officers. The mutineers attempted to persuade the sailors aboard the other ships in the harbor to join them, but the commanding admiral in Odessa quickly ordered the rest of the fleet out to sea. Confused and lacking effective leadership, the revolutionaries took the *Potemkin* to a Romanian port, where they scuttled the mighty vessel and escaped into the countryside. In August, the news that the elections to the Duma would be based on limited suffrage and that the new assembly would have only deliberative powers provoked increased popular agitation for universal suffrage and the establishment of the Duma as a legislative body. In September 1905 the liberal and democratic intelligentsia established a new political party, the Constitutional Democratic party (CDP).

Popular disaffection with the tsarist regime was spreading rapidly, and in October 1905 resentment turned into revolution. The All-Russian Railway Workers' Union called a general strike, and on October 25 all railway transportation in the Russian Empire came to a halt. All essential services ceased, and Russia's factories fell silent. In St. Petersburg, the workers took control of the city and held elections. On October 26, on the initiative of the members of the peasant-oriented Socialist Revolutionary party (SRS) and the Menshevik wing of the St. Petersburg RSDWP, they formed their own government, which they called the St. Petersburg Soviet [council] of Workers' Deputies. Trotsky was elected vice chairman of the soviet.

On October 30, with St. Petersburg at a standstill,

the tsar, under pressure from his more pragmatic advisers, began to make concessions. Count Sergey Yulyevich Witte, the architect of Russia's modernization program, was appointed prime minister. The tsar granted his people freedom of speech, conscience, and assembly, announced that the franchise for elections to the Duma would be widened, and promised a constitution. Most liberals thought the tsar's concessions adequate, but the soviet, now led by Trotsky, thought them purely cosmetic.

Lenin arrived in St. Petersburg on November 8, four days after the soviet called off the strike. While urging the Bolsheviks to prepare for an uprising, he promoted his assessment of the new form of assembly that had emerged from the revolutionary turmoil, declaring that the soviet should be considered the "provisional revolutionary government of all Russia."

Lenin's hopes for the establishment of a provisional revolutionary government were dashed in mid-December, when the authorities began arresting the soviet's members. A few days later, a general strike erupted in Moscow, rapidly turning into an armed insurrection that ended in abject defeat on December 31, by which time more than 1,000 working-class Muscovites, including 86 children, had been hacked to death by saber-wielding cavalrymen, shot by footsoldiers of the elite Semenevsky Guards, or blown apart by artillery shells.

While workers died in Moscow and the tsar's campaign to reassert his authority gathered momentum, Lenin and a group of Bolsheviks conferred in Tammerfors, Finland. Several of Lenin's colleagues charged him with moral responsibility for the Moscow debacle. Lenin rejected the charges, portraying the current situation as a dress rehearsal for future revolutions and asserting that the workers and the party had learned much of value from the events of the past few weeks.

In April 1906, by which time voting for the Duma had taken place in most parts of Russia, 62 Menshevik and 46 Bolshevik delegates met in Stockholm, Sweden, for the Fourth Congress of the

> *In practice Lenin had been historically the exclusive and unchallenged head of the party for many years. . . . The very thought of going against Lenin was frightening and odious, and required from the Bolshevik mass what it was incapable of giving.*
> —N. N. SUKHANOV

At the Fourth Congress of the RSDWP in 1906, Joseph Stalin, a Bolshevik from the Russian province of Georgia, wholeheartedly endorsed Lenin's defense of the policy of robbing banks to raise funds for the party. Stalin was a dedicated revolutionary with a pronounced capacity for ruthlessness.

RSDWP. The first issue on the agenda at the congress was the elections to the Duma, which the RSDWP and the recently founded Socialist Revolutionary party (SRP) had boycotted. (The SRP was basically a successor organization to the People's Will and Land and Freedom.) Of the 478 deputies elected, 190 were liberal Constitutional Democrats; 107 were members of a radical peasant organization called the Labor Group. The extent of mass participation in the elections had convinced the Mensheviks that the boycott was a mistake, and they ordered the formation of a Social Democratic slate in Transcaucasia, a province that had yet to vote. The Bolsheviks immediately attacked the Menshevik initiative, calling it a betrayal of the party's established revolutionary position. Then, to the horror of his own faction, Lenin announced that he supported the Mensheviks' decision. The Bolsheviks, he said, should acknowledge the interest the masses had shown in the elections. They should, he suggested, put up candidates, and those who secured election should use the Duma as a platform from which to encourage the masses to take political action outside the parliamentary arena. The Duma should be used in such a way as to expose its inadequacy as a democratic institution.

Another important issue discussed at the congress was the matter of revolutionary expropriations, or "exes" — illegal acts, such as bank robberies, conducted to raise funds for the party. In Lenin's view, "exes" were an acceptable activity, and he held to this position even though both wings of the party voted for termination of the "exes" and dissolution of the armed bands that engaged in them. Lenin's stand on this issue greatly impressed Joseph Stalin, a young Bolshevik delegate from the southern Russian province of Georgia. Stalin would eventually become a giant of the revolutionary movement in his own right.

In July 1906 the tsar ordered the Duma dissolved and announced that new elections would be held in January 1907. During the next few months, Lenin and his lieutenants continued to agitate for an armed uprising. While allowing the formation of a Bolshevik slate for the elections to the Second Duma, Lenin made it clear that he expected any Bolshevik who got elected to use his position to foment revolution. When the Second Duma opened in March 1907, Russia's new prime minister, Pyotr Arkadyevich Stolypin, who had succeeded Witte following the latter's resignation in 1906, quickly realized that the new assembly would be useless to the regime. Although there were 90 ultraconservative deputies who would undoubtedly support the government, they would face intense opposition from the 34 SRs and 65 Social Democrats — including 12 Bolsheviks — who had won election. Stolypin gradually became convinced that he should dissolve the Second Duma.

Discussion of the balance of forces in the Second Duma featured prominently at the Fifth Congress of the RSDWP, which took place in London in May. More than 300 delegates representing approximately 150 Social-Democratic groups throughout the Russian empire and abroad attended. Lenin won control of the central committee on a straight vote, with none of the machinations that had secured his original majority at the second party congress.

A citizen of Moscow stares at the body of a revolutionary killed during the street fighting that erupted there in December 1905. The tsarist authorities, faced with a general strike that had turned into an armed insurrection, decided to crush the local revolutionary movement by force.

Pyotty Arkadyevich Stolypin, was appointed prime minister of Russia in 1906. Determined to eradicate the Russian revolutionary movement, he masterminded a campaign of repression so severe that the hangman's noose became known as "Stolypin's necktie."

In June 1907 Stolypin found a suitable pretext for dissolving the Second Duma. A police spy obtained a copy of a secret Social-Democratic policy document recommending incitement of the army to mutiny. On June 16 Stolypin dissolved the Second Duma and ordered a major revision of the election laws to reduce the representation of opposition parties in future Dumas. To demonstrate further his intention to neutralize the opposition, Stolypin had most of the RSDWP deputies to the Second Duma arrested and sent to labor camps.

Shortly after the Fifth Congress of the RSDWP dispersed, Lenin's political fortunes began to decline, even though he had achieved a majority at the congress. Much to the surprise of his followers, Lenin recommended that the RSDWP should work within the Third Duma even though the radical opposition parties were now very much in the minority. The confusion felt by many Social Democrats at Lenin's latest pronouncement was nothing, however, compared to the anger that gripped them when they learned that the SPD had discovered that the Bolsheviks had shipped counterfeiting paper to the Berlin offices of an SPD newspaper without the German socialists' knowledge. The senior Russian Social Democrats were appalled by the Bolsheviks' cynical exploitation of Europe's premier socialist party.

Russian Cossacks, or cavalry troops, bed down in a mansion in the Russian section of Poland during their campaign against revolutionary groups in the summer of 1905. By that time public disaffection with the tsarist regime had reached critical proportions.

By the end of 1907, many of Lenin's closest colleagues had deserted him, citing among their reasons his contempt for majority opinion in his own faction and his willingness to seize for his own use funds intended for the party as a whole. Lenin's spirits fell still further as it became apparent that the campaign of repression masterminded by Stolypin had all but destroyed the revolutionary movement inside Russia. In December, Lenin and Krupskaya returned to Geneva, where they accustomed themselves once more to the émigré's existence. "All day," writes Krupskaya in *Reminiscences of Lenin*, "Vladimir Ilich sat in the library, but in the evening we did not know what to do with ourselves. It was difficult to sit in our uncomfortable, cold room. We longed for the company of human beings."

Lenin had arrived at the threshold of one of the loneliest and most difficult periods of his career. During this time, however, from the perspective afforded by his solitude, Lenin would continue to transform his ruling passions into truly revolutionary results.

Imprisoned in the aftermath of the Russian revolution of 1905, Trotsky awaits trial for his involvement with the St. Petersburg Soviet of Workers' Deputies. A form of workers' parliament, the *Soviet*, or council, had come into existence during the revolution. Lenin considered it "the germ of the provisional revolutionary government."

5

Preaching in an Empty Church

Shortly after arriving in Geneva, Lenin resurrected *The Proletarian*, a Bolshevik newspaper first published between May and November of 1905, and invited Trotsky and two other prominent Bolshevik writers, Maxim Gorky and Anatoly Lunacharsky, to contribute to it. Lenin also set to work editing a variety of other Bolshevik publications and writing numerous leaflets and pamphlets. Many of these dealt with the agrarian reform recently introduced in Russia by Stolypin, who hoped to achieve social and political stability in the countryside by means of a policy of land redistribution that was intended to exploit the peasants' innate conservatism, creating a new, property-oriented class of *kulaks* — moderately wealthy, independent farmers.

Lenin recognized that the peasants' susceptibility to revolutionary propaganda would decline as the new class developed. The revolutionary movement, which at this point was everywhere in disarray, now faced a race against time, he believed. Unless a new upheaval could be triggered before Stolypin's agrar-

> *As long as capitalism and Socialism remain, we cannot live in peace. In the end one or the other will triumph—a funeral requiem will be sung either over the Soviet Republic or over world capitalism.*
> —LENIN

Lenin in 1910, during one of the most difficult periods of his career. Government repression of the Social Democratic movement had proven remarkably effective, and many Social Democrats who had managed to avoid death or imprisonment were now becoming increasingly apathetic and depressed.

Lenin (left) plays chess with fellow Bolshevik Alesksandr Bogdanov at Maxim Gorky's villa on the Italian island of Capri in 1908. Although one of Lenin's closest political allies, Gorky was also one of his most critical.

ian policy had transformed the countryside, the revolutionaries would lose a vital base of support. Many other reforms implemented by Stolypin also threatened to alleviate the social discontent that fueled the flames of revolution. A national insurance system was established for the workers, compulsory elementary education was introduced, and civic equality was enforced.

At the end of 1908, Lenin and Krupskaya left Geneva for Paris, hoping that life in a cosmopolitan city would raise their spirits. A year later, however, he was still in low spirits. Adding to Lenin's depression was the fact that inside Russia, the Social Democrats were almost everywhere in retreat, hounded by police spies and increasingly prone to apathy. By 1909 the fortunes of the party had declined precipitously.

Lenin's steadfast refusal to moderate his position for the sake of party unity became a major subject of debate within the Second International. Lenin was campaigning particularly hard against the increasingly influential group of Social Democrats, known as liquidators, whose members advocated the liquidation of the party's underground organizations. The factional infighting that his intransigence on this and other issues generated at RSDWP meetings at the Second International's 1910 congress in Copenhagen, Denmark, appalled the western European socialists. In his *Three Who Made a Revolution*, historian Bertram D. Wolfe gives an account of a conversation between Akselrod and a member of the International Socialist Bureau — the Second International's coordinating body — that captures the essence of the gulf that separated Lenin from all Social Democrats, excepting his own followers. The official asked: "Do you mean to say that all these splits and quarrels are the work of one man? But how can one man be so effective and so dangerous?" Akselrod replied: "Because there is not another man who for twenty-four hours of the day is taken up with the revolution, who has no other thoughts but thoughts of revolution, and who, even in his sleep, dreams of nothing but revolution. Just try and handle such a fellow."

In January 1912 Lenin convened a small conference of his supporters from Russia and western Europe in Prague, then the capital of the western Austro-Hungarian province of Bohemia. As Lenin had planned, none of his opponents attended the conference, whose deliberations he directed with an iron hand from the outset. He persuaded the 14 voting delegates to designate the meeting a "general party conference" and "the supreme organ of the party," and to consider themselves present at a "Congress of the Russian Social Democratic Workers' Party." He then forced through a resolution stating that the party's former central committee had become defunct and secured the election of a new central committee composed of diehard Leninists. Lenin had thus taken what was, as British historian Edward Hallett Carr writes, "an unconstitutional step [that] clearly marked the claim of the Bolsheviks to form by themselves, and to the exclusion of all liquidators, Menshevik and other, the Russian Social Democratic Workers' Party. . . . Henceforth the Bolsheviks were no longer a faction within the party, but the party itself."

Lenin's coup touched off an explosion of protest throughout the Russian Social Democratic movement, whose various tendencies were unable, however, to devise a common response to this disturbing development.

During this period, Lenin's continuing criticism of the Mensheviks came to seem increasingly jus-

Russian Social Democratic émigrés fraternize in a Paris café in 1906. In the early 20th century social democracy was an international movement, and many dissidents came to Paris to take refuge from political oppression in their own countries.

Russian landowners meet to select their candidates for the elections to the Duma — the Russian parliament — in March 1907. The Duma was dissolved just three months later by Stolypin, who resented the election of almost 100 socialists.

tified as it grew apparent that in Russia's major industrial centers most workers favored the Bolshevik line. The fact that 80 percent of Russia's industrial workers, most of whom normally took a dim view of factionalism, had continued to support the Bolshevik newspaper *Pravda* even when, a few months after its inception in April 1912, Lenin began using it as a platform for violent attacks on his opponents, demonstrated that the workers were now more prepared than ever before to back the Social-Democratic revolutionary wing. Further proof of the workers' disaffection with Menshevism also emerged in 1912, with the elections to the Fourth Duma. In the industrial centers where the workers were allowed to nominate candidates, the Bolsheviks swept the board.

In July 1912, Lenin, Krupskaya, Grigory Yevseyevich Zinoviev, and Lev Borisovich Kamenev, another leading Bolshevik, moved to Cracow, a city in the Polish province of Galicia, which was then part of Austria-Hungary. The new location put them closer to the Russian border, thus shortening their lines of communication with the Bolshevik underground organization. In December, at a party council held in his home in Cracow, Lenin urged the delegates to organize strikes and street demonstrations, and to institute secret Bolshevik committees in the factories.

At this point, Lenin's place within the forces opposing the regime was, to say the least, paradoxical. The leading Mensheviks, who continued to claim, against all the evidence, that they enjoyed substantial support in the trade unions, had all but dismissed him as a blight on the face of democratic socialism. The workers themselves, however, a core element of the democratic movement, were now according his straightforward calls for revolutionary action an increasingly favorable response.

In July 1914 Lenin's activities were discussed at a conference of the International Socialist Bureau. Several leading western European and Russian socialists — including Plekhanov, Martov, Trotsky, and Rosa Luxemburg, a Polish-born member of the SPD who had an unshakeable faith in the revolutionary creativity of the masses and an intense dislike of bureaucracy — questioned a young French Bolshevik named Inessa Armand, whom Lenin, refusing to attend the conference himself, had sent to

Lenin loathed Russia's bourgeoisie, of which the socialites shown here in 1907 are typical examples. In 1917, when the Bolsheviks seized power in Russia, he announced that he and his party would "destroy the entire bourgeoisie, grind it to powder." He subsequently kept his promise.

Rosa Luxemburg, the Polish-born German socialist, was coauthor, with Lenin and Martov, of the 1907 resolution of the Second International. The resolution called on socialists everywhere "to utilize the economic and political crisis created by the war to rouse the masses and thereby to hasten the downfall of capitalist class rule."

speak on his behalf. Lenin's argument was that party unity would be achieved if the rest of the party would acknowledge Lenin's committee as the central committee of the whole party. In response, the Russian Social Democrats condemned Lenin yet again. They also convinced the International Socialist Bureau that the situation should be debated at the next congress of the Second International, which was scheduled for August. A few days later, however, the tensions between the great powers of Europe erupted into open conflict, plunging the Continent into a war that would change the entire world and destroy the Second International.

On July 28, 1914, Austria-Hungary declared war on Serbia. On July 29 Serbia's ally, Russia, mobilized her forces along her borders with Austria and Austria's ally, Germany. The German government declared war on Russia on August 1, and on Russia's ally, France, on August 3. That same day, German forces thrust into neutral Belgium on their way to invade France. Great Britain, which had pledged to assist Belgium, declared war on Germany on August 4. World War I had begun.

It was also on August 4, 1914, that the parliamentary representatives of the SPD betrayed their party's commitment to international socialism by voting approval of the German government's request for war credits, thus acting in direct contravention of a vital element of the resolution on war that the Second International had adopted at its 1907 congress in Stuttgart, Germany. That resolution had called upon socialist parties in all countries to do all they could to prevent a conflict, or, in the event that war broke out, to demand its immediate cessation. The SPD had set a fatal example. The leaders of the socialist parties of the other belligerent nations also aligned themselves with their national rulers, telling the workers they represented to fight and die as patriots.

The tragedy of August 4, 1914, was heightened by the fact that by then, the second of the Stuttgart resolution's last two paragraphs — which were drafted by Lenin, Luxemburg, and Martov — had largely been forgotten by the vast majority of the international socialist communists, and especially by its most prominent leaders. In time, however, events would force them to remember the contents of that paragraph. What Lenin, Luxemburg, and Martov had written reads as follows:

> "In case war should break out anyway, it is [the socialists'] duty to intervene in favor of its speedy termination, and with all their powers to utilize the economic and political crisis created by the war, to rouse the masses and thereby to hasten the downfall of capitalist class rule."

Seven years after the Stuttgart conference, only one leading European socialist would be guided by the spirit of the final paragraph: Lenin.

When Lenin read the first reports of the SPD's betrayal of the Stuttgart resolution, he thought the German government had concocted the story to convince its enemies that all of German society supported the war. Then, when he realized that the SPD had indeed reneged on its principles, he declared, "The Second International is dead."

Russian orthodox priests conduct funeral services for Russian soldiers killed in World War I. Lenin responded to the outbreak of hostilities in August 1914 by demanding that the conflict, which he saw as a clash between imperialist national bourgeoisie, be transformed into an international civil war between workers and capitalists.

Citizens of the Russian section of Poland are fed at a field kitchen while being evacuated to Russia at the beginning of World War I. Tensions mounted as the German army steadily advanced eastward, having inflicted a crushing defeat on the Russians at Tannenberg, East Prussia, in August 1914.

As a Russian national, Lenin was no longer welcome in Austria-Hungary. With the assistance of Victor Adler, the leader of the Austrian Social Democrats, he received permission from the Austrian authorities to leave for Switzerland, which was neutral. Shortly after arriving in Bern, Lenin began presenting his own ideas on what he considered the correct approach for socialists to the situation in Europe. He did not approve of Trotsky's demands for "peace without indemnities and annexations, peace without victors and vanquished." Lenin intended to live up to the principle expressed in the final paragraph of the Stuttgart resolution: to exploit the international crisis in the interests of revolution and to transform the imperialist war between the European bourgeoisies into an inter-

national civil war between workers and capitalists. At a debate in Zurich, Lenin proposed that the ordinary soldiers of every army engaged in the conflict should turn their guns on their own officers. This suggestion horrified many Russian Social Democrats. Even Plekhanov had proposed that socialists in Britain, France, and Russia had a duty to assist their governments in what he saw as a just fight against German militarism.

For Lenin, the fact that Europe's major socialist parties had succumbed to war fever and nationalism as enthusiastically as the bourgeoisie was a natural result of their revisionism. Their opportunistic willingness to abandon the revolutionary path in favor of working within the framework of bourgeois democracy had left them susceptible to bourgeois democracy's worst vices.

Lenin's basic recommendations on the war were published in the newspaper *The Social Democrat* on November 1, 1914. He attacked the leaders of the Second International for betraying the workers: "The proletarian International has not perished and will not perish. The working masses will overcome all obstacles and create a new International. . . . [It] is necessary to turn the weapons against the governments and the bourgeoisie of the respective countries. . . . Turning the present imperialist war into a civil war is the only correct proletarian slogan."

Although Lenin's position on the war made him extremely unpopular with socialists of all shades at first, the resounding moral victory he gained by keeping faith with his convictions would eventually give Bolshevism a decisive advantage in its struggle against both the forces of reaction and those socialist tendencies that lacked true revolutionary spirit. During the first three years of World War I, he would know great loneliness and unhappiness. Ultimately, however, this time of trial would prove to have hardened and sharpened the sword that Lenin had been fashioning for slaying tsarists and nonrevolutionary socialists alike since the beginning of his career.

Lenin savors the mountain air in Austro-Hungarian Poland, where he lived from 1912 until the outbreak of World War I. The Austrian government, which had declared war on Russia, then allowed him to leave for neutral Switzerland.

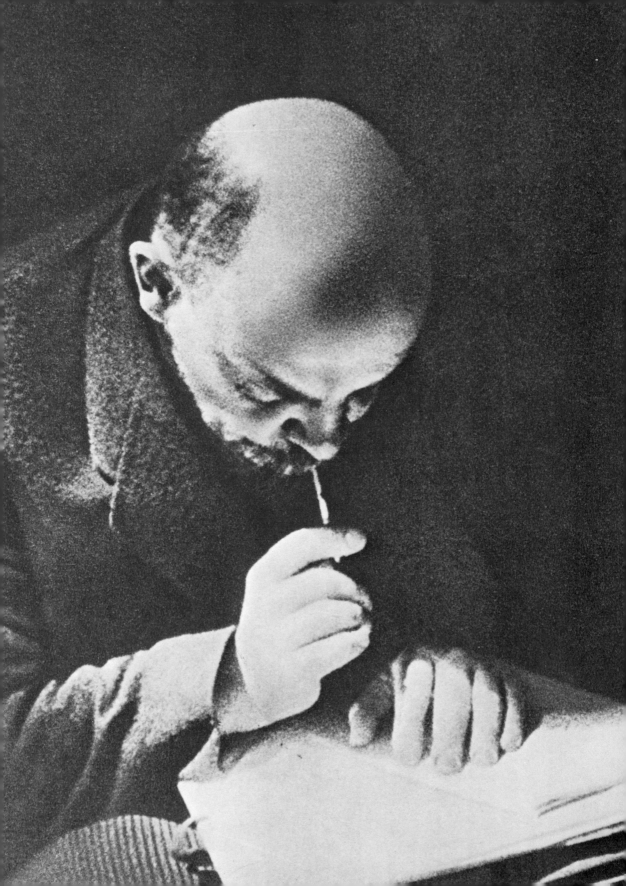

6

Prophet of the Popular Will

On September 5, 1915, 38 socialists from all European countries met in Zimmerwald, Switzerland, to discuss the implications of the war. Prior to the meeting, Lenin's proposal that a new, revolutionary and insurrectionary International be created and that an appeal be made to the workers and soldiers of the belligerent nations to go on strike against the war had met with a hostile reception from many Social Democratic émigrés. When Lenin made similar recommendations at Zimmerwald, he fared no better. The delegates eventually endorsed a manifesto, written largely by Trotsky and containing amendments drafted by a Bulgarian Social Democrat named Khristian Georgyevich Rakovsky.

The manifesto, which called for "peace without indemnities and without annexations" on the basis of the "self-determination of peoples," did not impress Lenin, who abstained from voting for its ratification. He continued to promote his own position on the war in the pages of *The Social Democrat*,

War is an inevitable part of capitalism. It is just as much a legitimate form of capitalism as is peace. . . . What idiot believes that the armed bourgeoisie can be overthrown without a struggle? It is simply insane to talk about abolishing capitalism without a frightful civil war or without a succession of such wars.
—LENIN

Lenin was not only an effective politician, but an immensely prolific writer. During his 30-year-long career, he wrote hundreds of books and pamphlets, as well as thousands of articles and letters. The fifth edition of his *Collected Works*, completed in 1965, contains almost 9,000 documents.

The five Bolshevik deputies to the fourth Duma, shortly after their arrest by the tsarist police in October 1914. They were arrested when authorities raided a conference at which the delegates were preparing to declare that Russia's workers would welcome the defeat of the tsarist regime by Germany.

emphasizing his contention that he wanted the war stopped by a socialist revolution throughout Europe that would enable Russia to proceed, without interruption, from the bourgeois revolution to the socialist revolution.

During this period, what little news reached Lenin from Russia seemed far from promising. The Bolshevik deputies to the Fourth Duma had been arrested in 1914 when the police raided a conference at which they were debating Lenin's demand that they make a public declaration that the workers wanted Russia to be defeated. The Mensheviks, retreating from their previous antiwar stance, now advocated a patriotic attitude toward the conflict in combination with demands for democratic reforms that Lenin and his colleagues considered mere palliatives. The Mensheviks had, in fact, remained wedded to the bourgeois values of nationalism and patriotism even though the plight of Russia's workers, the class whose interests they claimed to support, had worsened as the war progressed. A string of military defeats had resulted in runaway inflation, reduced wages, and widespread strikes. Worse yet, the desperate impoverishment of the workers existed alongside the high standard of living still enjoyed by the wealthy.

The tsar had anticipated a quick victory, but his forces were no match for the Germans. The outcome of World War I was to be decided by technology and training, and Russia was not equipped to produce such sophisticated military hardware as that possessed by the Germans. Many of Russia's soldiers had no weapons at all or lacked ammunition for the ones they did have. An astounding 4 million of them had been slaughtered or captured in the first 10 months of fighting.

In April 1916 the socialist international committee established at Zimmerwald held a conference in the Swiss town of Krenthal. Lenin's line on the war received a good deal more support than it had at Zimmerwald, and he and his colleagues in the radical grouping that had been dubbed the Zimmerwald Left, although they failed to secure majority endorsement of their views by the Krenthal delegates, did manage to persuade the conference to adopt a resolution censuring the International Socialist Bureau.

A Russian officer visits a military cemetery early in 1915, by which time 4 million Russian troops had been killed or captured. In June 1915, Lenin, anticipating greater revolutionary consciousness throughout Europe as a result of the conflict, wrote, "The experience of war . . . stuns and shatters some, but it enlightens and hardens others."

In January 1917, in an address to Swiss workers, Lenin portrayed Europe as "pregnant with revolution" despite the "graveyard silence" that had descended upon it. "The monstrous horrors of the imperialist war," he continued, "and the suffering caused by the high cost of living engender everywhere a revolutionary spirit." In conclusion, he said, "We, the old ones, may never live to see the decisive battles of the coming revolution."

Lenin's concern that the revolution might not take place in his lifetime proved entirely unjustified. Russia's situation was now absolutely critical. By the end of 1916, massive recruitment into the army had resulted in severe manpower deficiencies in agriculture and industry. The economy was on the verge of collapse. Inflation was rampant, the transportation system had broken down, and food and fuel were in desperately short supply. The situation was equally disastrous at the front. Of the nearly 15 million Russians mobilized since 1914, more than 5.5 million had been killed or wounded.

Workers in Kiev, the capital of Russia's Ukraine province, take to the streets to protest food and fuel shortages in March 1917.

By this time, the tsar had completely forfeited the confidence of his people. He was resolutely ignoring the crescendo of demands emanating from all social classes that he appoint a new, broad-based government containing leading members of the various political parties, enjoying the confidence of the Duma, and possessing full authority to organize industry and secure food supplies for the soldiers and workers.

On March 8, 1917, in the predominantly working-class Vyborg district of Petrograd — as St. Petersburg had been renamed in 1914 — women demonstrated to protest food shortages. They were soon joined by 50,000 engineering workers. By March 10, nearly 200,000 workers were on strike, marching in the streets to protest the food shortages and to voice their opposition to the war and the regime. The tsarist system, already shaken to its foundations by the turmoil of war, had begun to collapse. A general strike was in effect. The city was immobilized.

Citizens of Petrograd march in a funeral procession for soldiers killed during the revolution of March 1917. The victims had sided with the populace and fought against units that remained loyal to the tsar.

Russian soldiers from the armies at the front attend a meeting of the Petrograd Soviet of Workers' and Soldiers' Deputies in the immediate aftermath of the revolution of March 1917. During the revolution, more than 170,000 of the Petrograd garrison's 180,000 troops had joined forces with the city's workers.

On Monday, March 12, soldiers of the elite Volynskii Regiment, incensed at having been ordered to shoot at strikers, assassinated their commanding officer. The revolt within the tsar's army had begun. By March 14, 170,000 of Petrograd's 180,000 garrison troops had joined forces with the workers.

At the same time, in the Tauride Palace, an unofficial meeting of the Duma — which the tsar had dissolved on March 12 — constituted itself as the Provisional Committee of the Duma, while a group of pro-war Mensheviks and SRs, meeting in another wing of the palace, formed a provisional executive committee of the Petrograd Soviet of Workers' Deputies, and called upon the city's workers to hold elections. The soldiers who had joined the workers' cause came to the first meeting of the soviet and gave their own account of the recent incidents. The workers in the hall stamped and roared their approval, and, by a unanimous vote, the Petrograd Soviet of Workers' Deputies was renamed the Petrograd Soviet of Workers' and Soldiers' Deputies.

On March 15 the tsar abdicated, ending the 300-year-old Romanov dynasty. A new constitutional body, the Provisional Government, was then formed pursuant to an agreement that had been reached between the Petrograd soviet's executive committee and the Provisional Committee of the Duma (CDP). The Provisional Government received the qualified support of both the Mensheviks, who were effectively allied with the SRs, and the handful of senior Bolsheviks who were in Petrograd at the time. A liberal noble, Prince Georgy Lvov, led the Council of Ministers. Aleksandr Kerensky, a 35-year-old SR and the son of Fyodor Kerensky, the Samara *gymnasium* director who had written a testimonial for Lenin in 1887, was appointed minister of justice.

On March 16 the Provisional Government endorsed seven elements of the nine-point reform program that had been put forward by the soviet on March 14. The seven elements were as follows: no disarming or transfer of units of the Petrograd garrison; abolition of class, national, and religious discrimination; establishment of a popular militia; institution of democratic local administration; freedom of speech, publication, and strike; the establishment of a constituent assembly; and amnesty for all political prisoners.

Tsar Nicholas II reviews troops at the Winter Palace shortly before the revolution of March 1917, which toppled him from power and made Russia, in Lenin's words, "the freest country in the world."

Despite these revolutionary changes, many soldiers and workers soon became dissatisfied with the Provisional Government, mainly because it wanted to keep Russia in the war. For Lenin, to whom news of the upheavals in Petrograd had come as a complete surprise, the fact that Russia had now become — as he described it in an article in *Pravda* — "the freest country in the world" was welcome but far from ideal. The country's newfound freedom, he believed, would be hollow indeed if the workers went on dying in a savage and pointless war. His first telegram to supporters in Petrograd left no room for doubt concerning his position: "Our tactics: absolute mistrust, no support of new government . . . to arm proletariat only guarantee . . . *no rapprochement with other parties.*"

Lenin's frustration at finding himself far from home at this crucial point increased when the British and the French, despite the fact that the new Russian government, with which they were still technically allied, had proclaimed an amnesty for political exiles, refused to provide him with travel papers. Adding to his consternation was the fact that, just as he had expected, his lieutenants inside Russia had diluted the party line for fear of alienating the Bolsheviks from the rest of the socialist community. Stalin and Kamenev, who were now editing *Pravda* in Petrograd, had published editorials urging support for the Provisional Government, recommending that the Bolsheviks and the left-wing Mensheviks unite, and proposing that Russia should carry on fighting until peace negotiations between the warring powers could be arranged. *Pravda*'s sudden adoption of a conciliatory attitude stunned the Petrograd Bolsheviks, intellectuals and workers alike, and gave their opponents the impression that the party moderates must have won out over the Leninists.

Having had his requests for a transit visa rejected by the British and the French, Lenin sought the German government's assistance, even though the Russian foreign minister, CDP leader Pavel Milyukov, had announced that any Russian citizen traveling through Germany would face prosecution. Lenin, undeterred, negotiated a deal using as intermediaries a German socialist and businessman named Alexander Helphand — who had many friends in high places in Germany — and a Polish Social Democrat who worked as a Bolshevik agent in Sweden and had contacts at the German Embassy in Stockholm. Helphand's suggestion that Germany had much to gain from aiding the return to Russia of an influential revolutionary who advocated his country's withdrawal from the war roused the interest of several top German generals and diplomats.

On April 9, 1917, Lenin, Krupskaya, and 30 other Social Democratic émigrés set out from Zurich on the long journey back to Russia — and revolution. At the first stop inside Germany, they transferred to a special, single-car train provided by the German government. Under the terms of the deal that Lenin had negotiated, the railway car in which he and his entourage traveled through Germany had "extraterritorial" status, meaning that for purposes of the journey it was considered Russian territory, just as embassies in a country are treated as foreign territory by that country's government. The train was thus "sealed," in the sense that the returning exiles had no direct contact with any Germans during the journey. The only person permitted to talk with the two German army officers assigned to escort the émigrés was a citizen of neutral Switzerland, a Social Democrat named Franz Platten, who acted as a liaison. Lenin, relying on his legal expertise as well as on his political acumen, had insisted on this arrangement to minimize his vulnerability to the charges of collaboration with the Germans that he would undoubtedly face from his enemies back in Russia.

The sealed train took the exiles all the way north through Germany to Sassnitz, a port on the Baltic. From Sassnitz, they crossed by ferry to Sweden, and then continued on by train through Finland to Petrograd.

On April 16, 1917, Lenin arrived at Petrograd's Finland Station. Triumphal arches had been erected along the platform; banners inscribed with revolutionary slogans festooned the entire building. Companies of soldiers, sailors, and Bolshevik Red

> *During a revolution, millions and tens of millions of people learn in a week more than they do in a year of ordinary, somnolent life.*
> —LENIN

Guards stood at attention as a military band played. Lenin, who hated ceremonies, stepped down, rather stiffly, to the platform, where he was immediately surrounded by a group of cheering Bolsheviks, one of whom, Aleksandra Mikhaylovna Kollontay, the daughter of a tsarist general, presented him with a bouquet of flowers. A few minutes later, having spoken briefly to the honor guard, Lenin entered what had once been the royal family's waiting room. There, he was greeted by Nikolay Semyonovich Chkheidze, the Menshevik chairman of the Petrograd soviet. Chkheidze then gave a welcoming speech that appealed for unity between socialists and defense of the revolution against "every kind of attack both from within and from without."

Lenin simply ignored Chkheidze. He looked around the room, stared at the ceiling for a moment, fussed with his bouquet, and then, to everyone's consternation, turned his back on the official party and addressed the crowd, launching into a speech that changed the course of the revolution and history.

"Dear comrades, soldiers, sailors and workers," Lenin declared. "I am happy to greet in your persons the victorious Russian revolution! I greet you as the vanguard of the world proletarian army. The predatory imperialist war is the beginning of a civil war all over Europe. . . . Any day, if not today or tomorrow, the crash of the whole of European imperialism may come. The Russian revolution you have made has prepared the way and opened a new epoch. Hail the world-wide socialist revolution!"

In the eyes of all who heard this, Lenin seemed to have taken leave of his senses. Every other Marxist in the audience believed, of course, in the idea of the two-stage revolution. The Bolsheviks themselves, since 1905, had argued that the coming revolution would be bourgeois-democratic in nature. And Lenin himself, in all his writings prior to the March revolution, had anticipated that a considerable amount of time would pass between the impending bourgeois revolution and the proletarian, socialist revolution. Now, however, he had changed his position completely.

As Lenin's audience began to recover from its sense of shock, soldiers burst into the room, lifted Lenin onto their shoulders, and carried him out into the station square. There, searchlights blazing down from the Peter and Paul Fortress — where Aleksandr Ulyanov had been imprisoned while awaiting execution three decades before — played across a vast crowd of tens of thousands of people carrying torches and red banners. The soldiers placed Lenin atop an armored car, which moved off toward the Kshesinskaia Palace, which was now the headquarters of the Bolshevik central committee. At intervals along the route, the armored car came to a halt, and Lenin made further speeches, always ending with the words "Long live the world-wide socialist revolution!"

Shortly before Lenin's arrival in Petrograd, Kerensky had annoyed some of his ministerial colleagues during a meeting of the cabinet by interjecting, in a manner that indicated he found the situation almost humorous, the following comment: "Just you wait," he had said. "Lenin is coming. Then the real thing will begin." Those few words, spoken half in jest, would prove to have been prophetic.

Lenin's voice . . . was a "voice from outside." There had broken in upon us in the revolution a note that was not, to be sure, a contradiction, but that was novel, harsh, and somewhat deafening.
—NIKOLAY SUKHANOV
Russian writer

7

The Present Predicts the Future

Shortly after his arrival in Petrograd on April 17, Lenin addressed his party comrades at a meeting in the Kshesinskaia Palace. Several Mensheviks were also present. Russian writer Nikolay Sukhanov, who was at the meeting, recounts in *The Russian Revolution 1917: A Personal Record* that what Lenin had to say "startled and amazed not only me, a heretic, who had accidentally dropped in, but all the true believers. . . . It seemed as though all the elements had risen from their abodes, and the spirit of universal destruction, knowing neither barriers nor doubts, neither human difficulties nor human calculations, was hovering around Kshesinskaia's reception-room above the heads of the bewitched disciples."

Lenin condemned the entire content of the manifesto that the Petrograd soviet had recently published. Revolutionary democracy and freedom of speech, which the manifesto claimed had now come into existence, were nowhere in evidence, he said.

I detest and abhor people who arouse the dark instincts of the masses, no matter what names these people bear and no matter how considerable their service to Russia may have been in the past.
—MAXIM GORKY
criticizing Lenin

Lenin spent one month in hiding near Petrograd to avoid arrest by the Provisional Government, which had ordered his detention in July 1917. That August he entered Finland disguised as a Finnish railway worker.

ОСЛѢПШІЕ ВОИНЫ
ВОЙНА ДО ПОЛНОЙ ПОБѢДЫ
ДА ЗДРАВСТВУЕТЬ СВОБОДА!

Blinded war victims march in Petrograd in the spring of 1917, opposing Bolshevik demands that Russia withdraw from the war and negotiate a separate peace with Germany. The inscription on the banner at the front of the parade reads: "War until total victory. Long live freedom."

The "imperialist bourgeoisie" was still running the country and controlling the newspapers. He attacked the leaders of the soviet for their bourgeois advocacy of "revolutionary defensism"—for wanting to continue the war in order to defend the revolution. Then, provoking further uproar in an already profoundly agitated audience, he declared: "We do not need a parliamentary republic, we do not need bourgeois democracy, we do not need any government except the Soviets of Workers', Soldiers' and Poor Peasants' Deputies." Once again, Lenin was casting aside his previous orthodoxy, outlining a program that, in the eyes of most other socialists, was entirely inappropriate to the situation in Russia as they saw it, and to the opening stages of the bourgeois-democratic revolution.

Later that same day, at another meeting, Lenin elaborated on the program he had outlined earlier.

76

The momentous points he made in the course of his speech are now known to history as *The April Theses*. To the consternation of every orthodox Marxist in the room, he declared that Russia was now passing from the bourgeois revolution — which, as he explained in a *Pravda* article setting out the theses in full on April 20, "gave power to the bourgeoisie as a result of the insufficient consciousness and organization of the proletariat" — to the second stage of the revolution, which, "must place power in the hands of the proletariat and poorest sections of the peasantry." Lenin then urged that no support should be given to the Provisional Government, which he characterized as a "government of capitalists" and, as such, irredeemably imperialist.

As Lenin hammered home his assessment of the situation, the audience grew increasingly restless. Clarifying the meaning of his new revolutionary slogan, "All Power to the Soviets," Lenin asserted that the soviets — which were now springing up all over the country — were the only possible form of revolutionary government. He exhorted the Bolsheviks to concentrate on changing their current minority status in those organizations by patiently and systematically explaining to the masses the importance of eliminating from the soviets all bourgeois influence — by which he meant the Mensheviks and the SRs. Again rejecting parliamentary democracy,

Speaking in Petrograd on April 17, 1917, Lenin outlines his *April Theses*, a radical analysis of the situation then prevailing in Russia.

Lenin called for the creation of "a republic of Soviets of Workers', Poor Peasants' and Peasants' Deputies throughout the country, growing from below upwards." The police, the army, and the bureaucracy, he declared, should be abolished, and the standing army replaced by a people's militia whose officers' salaries should not exceed the average working wage. Lenin also demanded the nationalization of all privately owned land, the merging of all banks into a single, national bank, the control of production and distribution by the soviets of workers' deputies, the creation of a new, revolutionary International, and the changing of the party's name from "social-democratic" to "communist."

The extent to which Lenin's new position had alienated his colleagues became apparent, the day after the theses were published in *Pravda*, when the Petrograd committee of the Bolsheviks rejected the theses by a vote of 13 to 2.

Despite the fact that virtually the whole party had disassociated itself from his ideas, Lenin was not intimidated. He responded to his critics with a series of incisive and carefully argued articles and pamphlets. He gave many speeches, facing down his opponents with a fortitude that impressed even his most violent detractors. By May, Lenin's line had won majority approval.

Russian prime minister Aleksandr Kerensky (second from right) confers with his senior military commanders in November 1917, on the eve of the Bolshevik seizure of power. Shortly before the insurrection, Lenin announced that following Kerensky's ouster the Bolsheviks would then "set up a government that *nobody* will overthrow."

During this period, Lenin also contended that "dual power" — the simultaneous operation of the Petrograd soviet and the Provisional Government — was a political anomaly. Particular vindication of this view came in May, when CDP leader Milyukov declared that Russia would fight on with the Allies until Germany surrendered. The executive committee of the soviet immediately voted to call an international conference of working-class factions and parties that were prepared to support the soviet's call for peace without annexations or indemnities. It was now obvious that two governments — the Provisional Government, reflecting the will of the bourgeoisie, and the Petrograd soviet, which was more attuned to the will of the people — existed in Petrograd.

On July 1, 1917, the All-Russian Congress of Soviets organized a Petrograd demonstration, hoping that it would reveal popular support for the Provisional Government. To their horror, 90 percent of the banners carried by the 400,000 demonstrators bore slogans supporting the Bolsheviks — the Provisional Government's most bitter opponents.

Even when a coalition representing the Provisional Government and the soviet was established in May, Russia's political situation remained contradictory. When the socialist leaders of the Provisional Government and the Petrograd soviet offered U.S. President Woodrow Wilson's demands for peace without annexations in support of their contention that Russia, in alliance with the United States (which had entered the war on the Allied side in April), could bring about a truly democratic peace, the country's war-weary soldiers and starving peasants were not impressed. They found Lenin's straightforward demands for an immediate end to the war, along with his contention that only continuing with the revolution could save Russia, much more appealing.

In May, Lenin's position was further strengthened when Trotsky, who had been living in the United States at the time of the March revolution, returned to Petrograd and joined an independent social-democratic group known as the United Social Democrats. This group had previously distanced itself from the Bolsheviks and the Mensheviks, but with Trotsky's entry into the organization's ranks, the United Social Democrats quickly changed direction, and, mainly at Trotsky's urging, began to support the Bolsheviks.

After the tsar's abdication, people had expected miraculous changes, but conditions in the capital — and throughout the country — had continued to deteriorate. Life did not seem much different under the new, democratic government, and increasing numbers of people began to show interest in the propaganda of the Bolsheviks, the only socialist party that had refused to participate in a bourgeois-socialist coalition whose weakness was becoming increasingly apparent.

In June 1917, as disputes between the Bolsheviks and the pro-war SRs and Mensheviks intensified, Kerensky, now minister of war, responded to Allied pressure for substantive military action and ordered a major offensive. Britain, France, and the United States hoped that a Russian offensive would force the Germans to return to the Russian front the thousands of troops they had sent to reinforce their armies in France. Even though by this point the Imperial Army had suffered nearly 8 million casualties — a great deal more than any other Allied army — Kerensky and his colleagues in the Provisional Government believed that further action would somehow be good for the army's morale. Inevitably, however, the traditional problems of poor leadership and inadequate supplies quickly brought the offensive to a halt, and by the end of July the Germans were staging successful counterattacks. Morale in the army, which was already bad, plummeted. During the next four months, more than 2 million troops would desert.

That the Bolsheviks profited from popular distrust of the Provisional Government became particularly apparent on July 1, 1917, when, at the urging of Minister of Posts and Telegraphs Irakli Tsereteli — who was a Menshevik — and several other socialists who held high positions in the coalition, the All-Russian Congress of Soviets organized a mass

Operators at Petrograd's central telephone exchange attend to their duties following the occupation of their building by troops of the Bolshevik military revolutionary committee, November 7, 1917. At 12:00 A.M. that day, Trotsky informed the Petrograd soviet that the Bolsheviks controlled the entire city.

Soviet officials appraise the crown jewels of the deposed Romanov dynasty in the aftermath of the revolution of November 1917. In August 1918, Lenin, fearing that the counterrevolutionary army might liberate the tsar, ordered the royal family's execution.

demonstration intending to prove that the people supported the soviet, the congress, and, by implication, the government. To the organizers' horror, however, 90 percent of the banners lofted by the 400,000 workers and soldiers who took to the streets bore pro-Bolshevik slogans. Inscriptions supporting the government were almost nowhere to be seen.

On July 16, 1917, a series of major demonstrations commenced in Petrograd. On July 17 approximately 400,000 demonstrators demanded that the Petrograd soviet's SR and Menshevik leaders take power. At the same time, it became apparent that the leaders of the Bolshevik military organization, along with the pro-Bolshevik sailors based at the naval fortress at Kronstadt in the Gulf of Finland, favored an immediate armed uprising. Lenin, however, considered such an action premature.

Later that same day, when fighting between pro-Bolshevik and government forces erupted, many leading Bolsheviks decided they could no longer distance themselves from their supporters' actions simply because they thought them politically incorrect. By then, however, it was too late. On July 19, Kerensky, with the support of the SR and Menshevik leaders of the soviet, moved against the Bolsheviks, summoning loyal troops to the capital and ordering that Lenin, Kamenev, and Zinoviev be arrested. Kamenev was caught, but Lenin and Zinoviev managed to escape, fleeing the city to hide in the marshes near Razliv, a village a few miles from Petrograd.

During the next three months, Lenin kept himself informed of developments in Petrograd via Bolshevik couriers. At the same time, he worked on his book *The State and Revolution*. His basic thesis was that the overthrow of the bourgeoisie could only be achieved by the proletariat's becoming the ruling class. He wrote, "The revolution must not mean that the new class rules, governs, through the *old* state machinery, but that this class *smashes* that machinery, and rules, governs, through *new* machinery." Recognizing that the creation of such a state would provoke "violent reaction from the defenders of the old order," Lenin stressed that the new state apparatus's primary function would be to crush the oppressing class.

In October 1917, Lenin, who had been in Finland since August, returned to Petrograd, where popular support for the Bolsheviks had increased dramatically. Earlier that month, the Bolsheviks had won 350 seats out of 710 in the Moscow municipal elections; they also had majorities in the soviets of many important cities, including Petrograd.

On October 23, Lenin called a meeting of the Bolshevik central committee. With the full support of Trotsky, Lenin persuaded the committee to declare itself in favor of armed insurrection. On October 29 the Petrograd soviet, of which Trotsky was now president, established a military-revolutionary committee, which immediately began making military preparations for the uprising.

Lenin and his lieutenants were now ready to overthrow the Kerensky government. In a speech he gave shortly before the insurrection, Lenin made it plain

> *Perseverance, persistance, willingness, determination and ability to test things a hundred times, to correct them a hundred times, but to achieve the goal come what may—these qualities of the proletariat are a guarantee that the proletariat will conquer.*
> —LENIN

Military cadets loyal to the Provisional Government are besieged in Moscow in November 1917. Counterrevolutionary resistance ceased in Moscow on November 15, after a week of bloody street fighting.

that the Bolsheviks stood for a complete break with the past. Once Kerensky had been overthrown, he said, the Bolsheviks would "at once give the land to the peasants, reconstruct the democratic liberties and institutions maimed by Kerensky, and set up a government that *nobody* will overthrow."

Early on November 7, 1917, the military-revolutionary committee of the Petrograd soviet launched the insurrection. Thousands of insurgents seized the railway stations, post offices, telegraph offices, and banks. At noon, Trotsky announced that the revolutionaries had taken control of the capital. Kerensky had fled the city, and some government ministers and other counterrevolutionary elements in Petrograd had taken refuge in the Winter Palace. Later that day, Bolshevik troops stormed the Winter Palace, rapidly overwhelming the defenders, a motley force of socialists, conservatives, financiers, and military cadets. At the same time, hundreds of workers', soldiers', and sailors' deputies crowded into the marble halls of the Smolny Institute — formerly a fashionable school for the daughters of the nobility — to attend the Second All-Russian Congress of Soviets. When the message arrived from the Winter Palace that the Provisional Government had been toppled, Lenin strode to the rostrum.

The juncture of history, for which in the interests of socialism Lenin had built the most effective revolutionary party in the world, had arrived. When the thunderous applause that greeted his appearance subsided, he began to speak.

"Comrades," he declared, "the workers' and peasants' revolution, the need for which the Bolsheviks have emphasized many times, has come to pass.

"What is the significance of this revolution? Its significance is . . . that we shall have a Soviet Government, without the participation of a bourgeoisie of any kind. The oppressed masses will themselves form a government. The old state machinery will be smashed to bits and in its place will be created a new machinery of government of Soviet organizations. From now on there is a new page in the history of Russia, and the present Third Russian Revolution shall in its final result lead to the victory of Socialism. . . .

"We should now occupy ourselves in Russia in building up a proletarian Socialist state. Long live the world-wide Socialist revolution."

Bolshevik troops guard Petrograd's Smolny Institute, the headquarters of the Bolsheviks and the Petrograd soviet, after the overthrow of the Provisional Government. It was at the Smolny Institute, on November 8, 1917, that a triumphant Lenin announced: "We should now occupy ourselves in Russia in building up a proletarian Socialist state. Long live the world-wide Socialist revolution."

8

Action and Reaction

Russia's new rulers found themselves besieged within hours of seizing power. Shortly after the capture of the Winter Palace, more than 100 soldiers' deputies, right-wing SRs, and Mensheviks walked out of the All-Russian Congress of Soviets in protest against the Petrograd soviet's actions. In addition to the hostility of the moderate socialists, the Bolsheviks would have to confront sabotage by diehard tsarists. The question of withdrawal from the war also had to be addressed. Still, Lenin and his lieutenants moved swiftly to begin the process of rescuing Russia from crisis and turning her into the world's first workers' state.

On the evening of November 8, 1917, the All-Russian Congress of Soviets endorsed a document that Lenin had written demanding a democratic peace without annexations or indemnities. It then ordered the nationalization of the country's banking institutions, adopted Lenin's decree abolishing the private ownership of land, and proceeded to establish the first Soviet government, the Council of People's Commissars, or Sovnarcom, a 15-member all-Bolshevik executive body of which Lenin was made chairman. Lenin thus became the head of the new Soviet state.

To pass so quickly from persecutions and clandestine existence to power. . . . It makes one dizzy.
—LENIN

Standing at the foot of a plaster model for a government-commissioned statue of Marx and Engels, Lenin addresses a crowd in Moscow on November 7, 1918, the first anniversary of the Bolshevik revolution.

Lenin (seated at rear center) and his colleagues on the Council of People's Commissars, the first Soviet government, which came into existence on November 8, 1917. As chairman of the council, Lenin was also the head of the new Soviet state.

Feliks Edmuncovich Dzerzhinsky, the veteran Polish-born Bolshevik. Lenin appointed him head of the All-Russian Extraordinary Commission for Combating Counterrevolution and Sabotage, or *Cheka*, in December 1917. Under his ruthless leadership, the *Cheka* killed approximately 280,000 counterrevolutionaries between 1917 and 1922.

Two days later, on November 10, in response to attempts by forces loyal to the Provisional Government to achieve that body's restoration, Sovnarcom promulgated a decree limiting freedom of the press. At the same time, Lenin, acting in accordance with his belief that the bourgeois-democratic revolution had spent itself, closed down the newspapers of the SRs and the Mensheviks, whose contention that the revolution was still in its bourgeois-democratic stage he considered counterrevolutionary.

In December 1917 the Bolsheviks provided their opponents with further evidence of their intention to brook no opposition by establishing the All-Russian Extraordinary Commission for Combating Counterrevolution and Sabotage. Known as the *Cheka*, this organization became one of the most formidable institutions of the entire state apparatus, ruthlessly hunting down the enemies of the revolution. It was led by a dedicated, utterly incorruptible Polish-born veteran Bolshevik named Feliks Edmundovich Dzerzhinsky. Lenin, further demonstrating his determination to concentrate as much power as possible in the hands of the party, made the Cheka directly accountable to Sovnarcom.

The Bolsheviks' overall effort to advance the revolutionary cause and consolidate their position necessarily included negotiating an end to Russian involvement in the war. The conflict had nearly depleted the country's reserves of raw materials and manpower. By the end of 1917, the Germans had conquered large areas of Russian territory, including vast tracts of the Ukraine, one of Russia's richest agricultural regions. Lenin wanted immediate peace, no matter what the territorial loss and economic consequences, but Trotsky, now people's commissar for foreign affairs, wanted to delay negotiations with the representatives of German *Kaiser* (emperor) Wilhelm II, in hopes that revolution would erupt in Germany and that he would then be negotiating with a new, socialist government.

In taking this position, Trotsky acted in accordance with his theory of "permanent revolution," which he had first begun to formulate after the revolution of 1905. Trotsky rejected the idea that capitalism would have to develop to its fullest extent before socialism could be achieved. Under certain conditions, he believed, especially in a country like Russia, where the proletariat vastly outnumbered the bourgeoisie, progress toward socialism could be accelerated. Trotsky also maintained that socialism could not survive in one country alone, that if other nations of the world remained capitalist they could pose a threat to a flegling socialist state. A socialist Russia, then, would have to aid the spread of socialism to other countries.

Lenin, always pragmatic, said he thought it senseless to wait for a hypothetical German revolution to bring about peace when the Russian revolution, which was an accomplished fact, needed immediate peace if it was to survive.

In December 1917, shortly after Germany and Soviet Russia signed a preliminary 30-day armistice, a Soviet delegation arrived in the German-occupied Polish city of Brest-Litovsk to begin peace negotiations. The talks made little progress, and Lenin sent Trotsky there to head the delegation himself. The Soviet negotiators had been thrown into considerable disarray by Germany's demands for 350,000 square miles of Russian territory and an indemnity of 3,000 million gold rubles.

By February 23 the first round of talks had broken down, and the German army had resumed its attack, overrunning even more Russian territory. The Germans increased their demands. Lenin, against considerable opposition from his colleagues, con-

Trotsky, people's commissar for foreign affairs, takes a break from negotiating a separate peace with Germany in Brest-Litovsk, Poland, February 1918.

tinued to insist that there was no alternative to acceptance, and eventually secured majority approval of his position. On March 3, 1918, the Treaty of Brest-Litovsk was signed. Under the terms of the treaty, Russia lost 1.3 million square miles of territory, 44 percent of its population, 30 percent of its arable land, 27 percent of its state income, 75 percent of its iron and coal, and 9,000 of its 16,000 industrial concerns. Lenin resented the humiliating conditions of the treaty, but he believed that only peace could save the revolution.

During the period that witnessed the Brest-Litovsk negotiations, the Bolsheviks undertook many initiatives on the domestic front, ordering the institution of workers' control over all industrial enterprises, proscribing the leaders of the CDP because they were supporting the counterrevolutionary cause, abolishing the existing legal system in favor of a new judiciary whose members were to base their decisions on "revolutionary conscience and revolutionary conceptions of right," and mandating the establishment of a new military, which would be known as the Red Army of Workers and Peasants. It was also during this period that Lenin eliminated one of the most serious obstacles confronting the Bolsheviks' drive to consolidate their power — the Constituent Assembly, for whose convocation his own party, like all the other parties, had previously pledged its support.

The results of the elections to the assembly, which were held in November 1917, proved unfavorable to the Bolsheviks, who won only 168 of the 703 contested seats; the SRs gained 380 seats, the Left SRs 39, the Mensheviks 18, and the CDP — whose leaders had not yet been proscribed — 17. (The Left SRs,

German troops survey the bodies of Bolshevik troops killed by the Whites, or counterrevolutionary forces, in May 1918. By that time the Germans, despite having concluded a peace treaty with the Soviet government, were actively backing the Whites in several areas where the Bolsheviks were not in control.

a radical splinter faction of the SRP, was the only non-Bolshevik political grouping that supported Lenin's policies and participated in the Soviet government.)

Lenin did not allow the election results to slow the Bolshevik advance. The question of the Constituent Assembly, he believed, had to be considered within the context of class struggle; both the interests of the revolution and the form of government, based on the soviets, that the revolution had produced were more important than the technical rights of the assembly. This view was shared by a majority of the Bolsheviks.

On January 18, 1918, the Constituent Assembly held its first and only meeting. When a Bolshevik declaration sanctioning the existing system of government was rejected by a majority of 237 to 138, the Bolsheviks and the Left SRs walked out of the assembly; on January 19, Lenin ordered the Constituent Assembly dissolved.

During the spring and summer of 1918 it seemed that the beleaguered Russian Revolution might die in its infancy. Due to war damage and fuel shortages, the freight capacity of the Russian railway system had fallen from its 1913 level of 10 million tons to 3 million tons, making the transportation of food from the rural areas to cities very difficult. What did reach the towns had often perished by the time it arrived. Russia's peasants, confronted with the decreasing value of the currency and the fact that there were few industrial goods to exchange for their produce, became unwilling to grow any more food than they needed to feed themselves. As a result, starvation crippled the cities, where workers were already suffering the ravages of unemployment as factories closed for lack of raw materials.

It was also during the spring and summer of 1918 that the Soviet government faced the first onslaught of the White, or counterrevolutionary, armies. These had been formed from the remnants of the Imperial Army by its most reactionary generals, who opposed the Soviet order and the separate peace. The Allied powers, angered by the Soviet government's decision to take Russia out of the war, not

The state is an institution built up for the sake of exercising violence. Previously this violence was exercised by a handful of moneybags over the entire people; now we want . . . to organize violence in the interests of the people.
—LENIN

Soviet and German diplomats negotiate the Treaty of Brest-Litovsk in March 1918. Registering their opposition to the treaty's terms, the Soviet Delegation stated that "the Soviet government . . . unable to resist the armed offensive of German imperialism, is forced to accept the peace terms to save revolutionary Russia."

only sent the Whites weapons and money, but intervened directly in the Soviet state's internal affairs. More than 50,000 Allied soldiers — British, American, Italian, Serbian, Polish, French, and Japanese — were sent to join the capitalist crusade to overthrow the revolution.

The job of leading the defense of the Russian Socialist Federative Soviet Republic (RSFSR), as Soviet Russia was now known, against the Whites and the Allied interventionary forces was given to Trotsky, who had been appointed people's commissar for war. Displaying remarkable organizational ability and immense personal courage, he succeeded in transforming an undisciplined mass into an army strong enough to defend the revolution. By January 1920, the Red Army numbered more than 5 million. Like the Cheka, which also expanded as the civil war continued, the Red Army was an instrument of the central government, subject to no popular control.

During the spring of 1918, shortly after the government had relocated from Petrograd to Moscow, which was further from the fighting fronts, the Bolsheviks — who were now known as the Russian Communist party (Bolsheviks), or RCP(B) — began to institute a program that became known as "war communism." This was designed to put the economy on a war footing, to establish communist society in Russia, and to issue state control over agriculture, thereby turning the peasantry into an agricultural proletariat. In order to feed the Red Army and the urban populations, the government authorized armed workers' commandos to requisition grain and other crops from the *kulaks*. The program remained in place until 1921.

As the civil war intensified, so too did economic centralization. The government rescinded the decree on workers' control, reestablished disciplinary management, extended the working day, sent the workers wherever they were needed, and imposed heavy fines and other penalties for absenteeism.

War communism was an extreme response to an extreme situation. The Bolsheviks were as determined to advance the revolution as its opponents were to destroy it. Always at the very center of this great feat of resistance on all fronts — military, economic, political, and diplomatic — was Lenin, leading his government and his party with determination and vigor. Never shrinking from his awesome responsibilities, unafraid to make difficult, even harsh decisions, he remained infallibly decisive throughout the 19-hour days he worked in his Moscow office.

During the summer of 1918, anti-Bolshevik uprisings increased. In response, Lenin initiated an expansion of the Cheka's already considerable campaign of mass terror against those who did not support the revolution. In June, the Left SRs, who had resigned from the government in protest against the Treaty of Brest-Litovsk, demanded an end to grain

Bolshevik troops patrol Petrograd in November 1917. Reorganization of those sections of the Russian military that supported the Soviet government accelerated in 1918 as the civil war escalated.

Moses Uritsky, the Petrograd *Cheka* chief, was shot by an anti-Bolshevik student on August 30, 1918. That same day, in Moscow, an attempt was made on Lenin's life.

requisitioning, the dissolution of the Red Army and the Cheka, and a revolutionary war against Germany. Lenin, angered by this questioning of policies and institutions integral to the survival of the revolution, had several leading Left SRs arrested. In July, when the Left SRs assassinated the German ambassador in Moscow, hoping to provoke German military retaliation, and to launch an anti-Bolshevik revolt, Lenin ordered the execution of 20 Left SR hostages.

Lenin still feared that the tsar might be freed by counterrevolutionary forces and restored to the throne. The imperial family was in Ekaterinburg, a city in the Ural Mountains, where they had been taken by the Bolsheviks following the fall of the Provisional Government. On July 16, 1918, Nicholas, his wife, Alexandra, his 14-year-old son, and his four daughters were shot by Bolshevik troops on Lenin's orders. "The execution of the tsar's family," Trotsky wrote in his diary many years later, "was needed not only in order to frighten, horrify, and dishearten the enemy, but also in order to shake up our own ranks, to show them that there was no turning back, that ahead lay either complete victory or complete ruin."

On August 30, 1918, Fanya Kaplan, a right-wing SR, approached Lenin as he was leaving a labor rally, pulled a pistol from under her coat, and fired twice, hitting him in the neck and shoulder. Lenin's doctors examined him and assured his colleagues that he was not as badly hurt as had at first been feared. Kaplan was executed three days later.

The day that saw the attempt on Lenin's life also witnessed the assassination of Moses Uritsky, chief of the Petrograd Cheka, by an anti-Bolshevik student. On the night of August 30, the Soviet government issued a decree ordering the working class "to respond to attempts on the life of its leader by still further consolidating its forces and by a merciless mass terror against all enemies of the revolution."

The use of terror became an integral element of Bolshevik strategy. The seeds of its institutionalization were sown six days after the attempt on Lenin's life, when a government decree expanded the powers of the Cheka, ushering in the massive campaign of intimidation officially labeled the "Red Terror."

It is estimated that by October 1922, when it was replaced by the State Political Administration (GPU), the Cheka had killed approximately 140,000 people by execution, and another 140,000 while putting down uprisings.

Many historians have analyzed the Red Terror in great detail while failing to deal with its corollary — the "White Terror." Some perspective on this troubled issue may, perhaps, be gained from the following single fact: In Finland, which proclaimed independence from Russia in July 1917, White forces under Carl Gustaf von Mannerheim, a former lieutenant-general in the Imperial Army, killed almost 100,000 workers, or roughly 25 percent of the entire Finnish proletariat, in just two months — April and May—in 1918.

Throughout January and February of 1919, Lenin prepared for the First Congress of the Communist International, or Comintern, an organization dedicated to the overthrow of capitalism throughout the world. Lenin attended every meeting of the first congress of this organization, which was held that March. The Comintern's program split the European socialist parties, separating the revolutionaries from the revisionists and reconstituting the former as communist parties under Soviet control. Lenin secured endorsement of his "Theses and Report on Bourgeois Democracy and the Dictatorship of the Proletariat." In this document, he declared that "the chief task of the communist parties in all countries where soviet government has not been established" would be to persuade the workers that "the new, proletarian democracy . . . must replace bourgeois democracy and the parliamentary system."

During the final months of 1919 and the first months of 1920, the Red Army won several victories over the Whites, whose lack of any coherent political program was by now alienating both their Allied backers and many of the very people to whom they presented themselves as liberators.

Lenin reads a copy of *Pravda* (*Truth*), the official newspaper of the Russian Communist party (Bolshevik), or RCP(B), in his Moscow office. Lenin relocated his administration from Petrograd to Moscow — which then became the Soviet capital — in the spring of 1918.

In the aftermath of the Red Army's invasion of Poland in 1920, Soviet troops and their camp followers languish in a Polish prison camp. Lenin's plan to bring socialism to Poland by force, and then to carry the revolution into western Europe, ended in abject failure.

Lenin leaves a meeting of trade unionists in Moscow accompanied by Krupskaya, who was appointed deputy people's commissar for education following the establishment of the communist government in 1917.

On April 22, 1920, Lenin's 50th birthday, the Moscow committee of the RCP(B) staged a rally to mark the occasion. Lenin, with typical modesty, waited until his supporters had finished their laudatory speeches before making an appearance. Even then, he attended only for a few minutes, and spoke but briefly. "Comrades," he declared, "I must thank you for two things: for today's greetings and even more for excusing me from listening to the anniversary speeches." Lenin, in fact, felt awkward when praised by his colleagues or feted in the press. He would, to some extent, have liked the Bolsheviks to be capable of existing as a leaderless party, as a perfectly collective organization.

Also in April 1920, the armies of Poland, which had been reconstituted as an independent republic in 1918, invaded the Ukraine, where a Bolshevik regime had been established following Germany's surrender and withdrawal. Poland's leader, Marshal Józef Piłsudski, had concluded a pact with Ukrainian nationalist Symon Petlyura, leader of the anti-Soviet forces in the Ukraine, whereby Poland would receive a portion of Ukrainian territory in return for helping Petlyura unseat the local Bolsheviks. In May, Soviet forces under General Mikhail Tukhachevsky pushed the Poles back to their own borders.

Lenin viewed Tukhachevsky's successes as an opportunity to carry the revolution west through Poland, on into neighboring Germany, and thus to western Europe. Convinced that if the Red Army drove the Poles all the way to Warsaw, the Polish capital, the Polish proletariat would overthrow the Piłsudski government and welcome the Soviets, Lenin ordered the army to keep advancing. However, instead of taking Warsaw, the Red Army lost a bloody battle at its gates and was then driven back.

By the end of 1920, the civil war was over. The Bolshevik government had not been toppled, but Lenin and his colleagues knew that the fight to save the revolution had eroded the party's ability to provide the effective leadership required for the country to recover from the ravages of war and proceed toward socialism. The RSFSR and the other soviet socialist republics, or SSRs, that would unite as the

Union of Soviet Socialist Republics (USSR) in December 1922, had been militarized, with the RCP(B) forced into the role of a general staff.

The devastation was of staggering proportions. Deaths resulting from the civil war exceeded those Russia had sustained in World War I. About 4 million Russians had died in the latter conflict; more than 8 million had died in the former, with around 7.25 million of those deaths having been caused by starvation. In 1917, the proletariat, the Bolsheviks' dictator class and core base of support, had numbered 3 million; by the end of 1920, it numbered less than 1.5 million. Those who had been lost were either killed in the war or had fled to the countryside in search of food, never to return. A generation of politically conscious workers had been decimated. Because of severe drought the harvest of 1920 had been a poor one, and the following year would bring another. By 1922, 5 million more lives would be lost.

Amidst the chaos, the Bolsheviks were, however, in possession of at least a measure of popular support, despite much hesitancy and disaffection on the part of various sectors of society during the war years. They had forged a tangible new state whose effectiveness was not in doubt. But, for Lenin and his colleagues, whether they would be able to preserve and strengthen it remained uncertain. The party itself seemed on the verge of a split, and this was a time when unity was essential. A faction that called itself the Workers' Opposition, led by Kollontay and People's Commissar for Labor Aleksandr Shlyapnikov, wanted a reversion from the central direction of production and virtual militarization of labor that had been major features of policy in the war years and a return to the direction of production by the trade unions. The Workers' Opposition also wanted all non-worker elements expelled from the party. Another group, the Democratic Centralists, were openly attacking Lenin's interpretation of democratic centralism.

That the desperate situation in the party and in the country called for an effective and coherent response was obvious to everyone. It would be Lenin who would rise to the occasion.

In 1919 Lenin delivered an address in Moscow's Red Square at a ceremony marking the dedication of a monument to Stenka Razin, a Cossack who led a rebellion against Tsar Alexis I Mikhaylovich in 1670–71.

9

Aftermath and Afterthoughts

Early in 1921, relations between the RCP(B) and the working class, which were already severely strained, took a sudden turn for the worse. Bad weather had been holding up deliveries of food to the cities, and the government had reduced the already meager bread ration by 30 percent. At the beginning of February, with food supplies in Petrograd almost exhausted, the Petrograd soviet's executive committee, of which Zinoviev was head, imposed martial law throughout the city to forestall bread riots. The workers immediately went on strike.

At first, the strikers issued demands concerning their economic grievances, asking for distributions of clothing and requesting official permission to send foraging parties to the countryside. Soon, however, influenced by Menshevik agitators, they began to demand the restoration of political liberties. Zinoviev and his colleagues managed to regain control of the situation at the end of the month, mainly by increasing the rations of soldiers and workers. The next explosion of protest, however, almost wrecked Bolshevik rule.

The worst thing that can befall a leader of an extreme party is to be compelled to take over a government in an epoch when the movement is not yet ripe for the domination of the class that he represents.
—FRIEDRICH ENGELS

Lenin and Krupskaya at their home in Gorki, in the summer of 1922, shortly after the Soviet leader suffered his first stroke. Despite Lenin's doctors trying to dissuade him from receiving business associates, Lenin made every effort to conduct business as usual.

Russian painter Isaak Brosky sketches Lenin at the Third Congress of the Comintern in July 1921. During his years in power, the humble Soviet leader repeatedly complained about the ever-increasing prevalence of his image in homes, offices, and factories. On one occasion, he declared: "And these portraits? Everywhere! What is the purpose of all this?"

In March 1921 the soviet representing the sailors at the Kronstadt naval base initiated a revolt against the government. Some of the rebels had participated in the storming of the Winter Palace in 1917, and around 75 percent of them were the sons of peasants and thus keenly aware of the situation in the countryside. They demanded an end to grain confiscations, reestablishment of the secret ballot, freedom of speech and of the press for all socialist groups, and independence for the trade unions. Hatred of war communism lay at the heart of the sailors' disaffection, and they blamed the government for all the problems then afflicting the country, ignoring the fact that the problems had arisen from the civil war.

For Lenin, the first order of the day was to crush the revolt, which was actually in progress when the Tenth Congress of the RCP(B) opened in Petrograd on March 8. Under the command of Tukhachevsky, elite Red Army and Cheka units, accompanied by several senior party leaders who left the congress to take part in the battle, marched across the frozen Gulf of Finland in the face of machine gun fire and artillery bombardments. A terrible massacre ensued, and the Kronstadt sailors were annihilated.

Even as the battle progressed, Lenin, speaking at the congress, put forward a plan for national regeneration called the New Economic Policy (NEP), which would entail the abolition of war communism, the prohibition of grain seizures, and the institution of a tax in kind for the peasants, which meant that the state would take only a fixed quota of their produce, leaving them free to sell any surplus on the open market. Lenin thus opened the way to a revival of legal private trade. His new policy was, in essence, a response to appalling economic circumstances, but a majority in the party and in the party leadership, recognizing that NEP represented the only guarantee of national recovery, gave it their wholehearted support. Lenin realized that NEP was a retreat from communism, but acted to preserve the successes the revolution had achieved.

Lenin's realism, foresight, and decisiveness saved the revolution, the economy, and the party. The beneficial effects of NEP on the economy were almost instantaneous and impressively dramatic. The relaxation of economic controls effected under NEP was accompanied by a loosening of the government's hold over social and cultural life.

Amid the increased social, cultural, and economic freedom occasioned by NEP, Lenin took great care to ensure that there would be no relaxation in the

Nurses tend to peasants suffering from malnutrition at a hospital in Samara in 1922, by which time the massive famine resulting from poor harvests in 1920 and 1921 had claimed the lives of 5 million Soviet citizens.

Lenin strolls in a park near Gorki in August 1922, while still recovering from his first stroke. It was at this time that Stalin, now general secretary of the RCP(B), began to take advantage of Lenin's absence from Moscow, securing control of the party machine.

By the end of 1922, Stalin had grown sufficiently confident of his ability to render the ailing Lenin politically ineffective. He therefore pursued a chauvinistic policy toward a number of soviet socialist republics even though he knew that Lenin strongly disapproved.

political sphere. At the Tenth Congress of the RCP(B), he called for a ban of all factions within the party and for harsh measures that would ensure that the only kind of political debate affecting the country would be that conducted within the ruling party. As a result, the Mensheviks and the SRs were outlawed.

The Eleventh Congress of the RCP(B) was the last one Lenin attended. At the congress, Joseph Stalin was elected general secretary of the party by the party central committee. Two months later, in May 1922, Lenin suffered a stroke. He would not be well enough to return to work until October.

Party leadership now passed to a triumvirate composed of Zinoviev, Kamenev, and Stalin, who now began using his position to push his own supporters — most of whom were, like Stalin himself, anti-intellectual and unimaginative with a tendency toward careerism — into leadership posts. At the same time, the bad feeling that had long characterized relations between the flamboyant, articulate Trotsky and the dour Stalin became more pronounced. The party itself had changed dramatically since 1917, in ways that boded ill for the future and left Trotsky increasingly alienated.

As Lenin recovered from his stroke, he began to realize what Stalin was doing, and managed to keep track of the situation in the party. In September 1922 Stalin drafted a resolution on relations between the RSFSR and five other SSRs that treated the government of the RSFSR as the government of those SSRs too. Lenin was appalled. Stalin's initiative violated the concept of equality between SSRs that Lenin had originally intended to prevail. To Lenin, this development demonstrated the extent to which the party was infected with the Great Russian chauvinism, or domineering nationalism, that had been a hallmark of tsarism. He would not, however, have an opportunity to intervene directly against Stalin. During the night of December 22–23, Lenin suffered another stroke, and became paralyzed on his right side.

Realizing that he might have only a little time left to live, Lenin addressed what he saw as the main problems confronting the party and the leadership. The series of notes for the next party congress that he dictated on this subject between December 23 and December 31, 1922, with a supplement dictated on January 4, 1923, are known as Lenin's "Testament." One of his main concerns was the continuing prospect of a split between the proletariat and the peasantry. This problem, however, was not of an immediately threatening nature. Lenin's most urgent concern was the possibility of a split in the party due to tensions within the leadership, specifically between Stalin and Trotsky.

On March 9, Lenin suffered a third stroke, which left him almost completely incapacitated and incapable of speaking. In May 1923 he was moved to a mansion in Gorki, a country town 30 miles from Moscow. By July, his health had begun to improve, and he was making considerable progress in learning to speak again. In October, he paid a fleeting visit to Moscow to see an agricultural exhibition. It was his last visit to the city. On January 21, 1924, his condition suddenly deteriorated, and at 6:50 PM on that same day, Vladimir Ilich Lenin died, at age 53, of a cerebral hemorrhage.

Lenin, shortly before he died at his Gorki home on January 21, 1924. Six days later, he was buried in a vault beneath a wall of the Kremlin. In 1930 the Soviet government authorized the construction of the mausoleum in Moscow's Red Square, where Lenin's body rests to this day.

This monument to Lenin in Chelyabinsk, Siberia, is one of hundreds of similar edifices that the Soviet government built following Lenin's death. Shortly after Lenin died, Krupskaya, who knew that her husband considered personality cults distinctly un-Marxist, wrote: "Do not raise memorials to him . . . to all this he attached so little importance in his life."

On January 23, Lenin's body was taken to Moscow. There, it lay in state in the House of Trade Unions, where hundreds of thousands of workers from all over the country came to pay their last respects. On January 26 the Second All-Union Congress of Soviets held a solemn ceremony in honor of the dead leader. Stalin's speech, unlike Krupskaya's, which was simple and straight from the heart, and Zinoviev's, which was dry and mechanical, was more like a religious prayer than a funeral oration. At the congress, decisions were taken to change the name of Petrograd to Leningrad, to make the anniversary of Lenin's death a day of national mourning, to erect monuments to Lenin in the country's major cities, to publish a collected edition of his works, and to preserve his body in a mausoleum.

On January 27 Lenin's coffin, draped in a red flag, was moved to a platform in Moscow's Red Square, close to the vault where it would remain until the mausoleum was ready. The entire square was a sea of red flags, and packed with hundreds of thousands of people wearing mourning bands edged with red. At 4:00 PM, in Moscow and in every city in the country, factory sirens sounded and artillery fired in salute. The thunderous tribute lasted three minutes, during which time Stalin, Zinoviev, Kamenev, Dzerzhinsky, Bukharin, and three other Bolsheviks carried Lenin's coffin down into the vault.

Shortly before Lenin died, Trotsky and 45 other party members had opened a struggle for greater democracy within the party. Stalin, who had effectively secured control of the party machine, saw to it that the pro-democracy group was condemned and that Trotsky was removed from his post as people's commissar for war. In 1928, Trotsky was deported from the USSR on Stalin's orders.

Stalin's first Five-Year plan, an enforced social revolution aimed at developing heavy industry and organizing a centrally directed agrarian economy

Trotsky, whom Stalin banished from the USSR in 1929, works at his home in Mexico City. In 1940 he was murdered by a Soviet agent acting on orders from Stalin, who, according to Trotsky, had perverted socialist democracy and the principles of Leninism.

based on collective farming, went into effect that year. To these ends, the kulaks were beaten into acquiescence to state policy by a campaign of official coercion and terror that greatly exceeded even the worst excesses of war communism. By March 1930, six million peasant deaths had resulted from the rupturing of the agricultural system caused by the collectivization drive.

In 1934 Stalin moved to consolidate his dictatorship over the party through terror. Between 1934 and 1939, he ordered the execution or deportation to labor camps of tens of thousands of party members. Also during that period, as part of Stalin's campaign against so-called enemies of the people, about 8 million Soviet citizens were arrested, of whom perhaps 800,000 were executed, while a large proportion of the remaining 7 million died in labor camps. Statistical data on the number of deaths resulting from Stalin's purges are scarce, but estimates range from 5 to 10 million.

Three Soviet women who played active roles as fighters and agitators during the Russian revolution of 1905 scrutinize a book about that momentous year in 1930. By that time Stalin had ruthlessly made himself absolute dictator of the USSR.

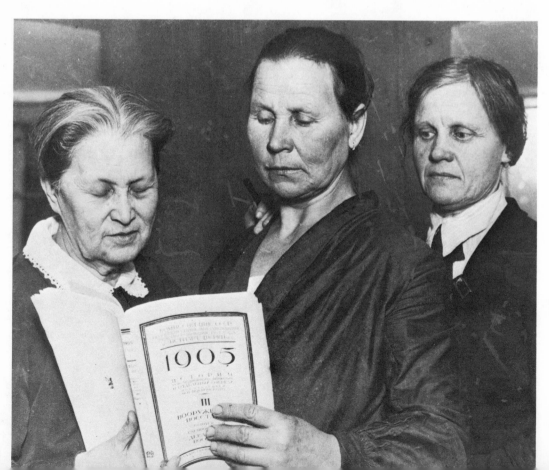

This monument to Lenin stands before the Smolny Institute in Petrograd, where on November 8, 1917, Lenin enunciated the basic elements of his vision for the world's first workers' state. All that he had hoped for was almost destroyed by Stalin, but the essence of his vision is now being rediscovered by the USSR's present leaders.

Many historians have claimed that Leninism and Stalinism were essentially the same or, at least, that Stalinism can be viewed as a logical development of Leninism. Whereas others, including many non-leftists, have rejected the idea. Lenin was undoubtedly one of the greatest leaders, most effective revolutionaries, and most powerful minds of his time. His ultimate aim was always the realization of a true producers' democracy, an egalitarian socioeconomic order promising real social harmony. As he himself stressed repeatedly, the worldwide realization of the kind of society that was at the heart of his vision would mean an end to war and an end to the exploitation of man by man. Men have seized power for worse ends than this.

Further Reading

Appignanesi, Richard. *Lenin for Beginners.* New York: Pantheon, 1979.

Fitzpatrick, Shelia. *The Russian Revolution 1917–1932.* Oxford: Oxford University Press, 1982.

Garza, Hedda. *Leon Trotsky.* New York: Chelsea House Publishers, 1986.

Liebman, Marcel. *Leninism under Lenin.* London: The Merlin Press Limited, 1980.

Schapiro, Leonard. *The Russian Revolutions of 1917: The Origins of Modern Communism.* New York: Basic Books, 1984.

Ulam, Adam B. *The Bolsheviks: The Intellectual, Personal and Political History of the Triumph of Communism in Russia.* New York: Macmillan, 1965.

Chronology

April 22, 1870	Born Vladimir Ilich Ulyanov (Lenin) in Simbirsk, Russia
May 20, 1887	Vows revenge against governmental system after eldest brother executed for plotting against the tsar
Dec. 1887	Expelled from Kazan University for attending student demonstration
1888	Studies and adopts Marx's theories
Nov. 1891	Passes his exams and becomes a lawyer
1893	Relocates to St. Petersburg to begin political revolutionary career
Dec. 20, 1895	Arrested for publishing revolutionary pamphlets
Feb. 1897	Exiled to Siberia for three years
March 1898	Russian Social Democratic Workers' party (R.S.D.W.P.) formed
1899	Lenin writes first article under name Lenin
July 29, 1900	Ends exile and starts *Iskra*, new newspaper for R.S.D.W.P.
1901	Writes *What Is To Be Done?*
Aug. 1903	Procedural disputes split R.S.D.W.P. into Lenin's "hard left" Bolsheviks and Martov's "moderate" Mensheviks
Jan. 22, 1905	"Bloody Sunday"; soldiers kill hundreds of workers leading a peaceful march for better working conditions
1907	Leaves for Germany after plans for revolution stall
Jan. 1912	Stages Bolshevik takeover of R.S.D.W.P.
Aug. 1914	World War I begins
March 1917	Nicholas II abdicates, Provisional Government takes power
Nov. 7, 1917	Bolsheviks overthrow Provisional Government
Nov. 8, 1917	Lenin becomes chairman of new government, the Council of People's Commissars
Nov. 11, 1917	World War I ends
March 3, 1918	Soviet government signs separate peace with Germany
Aug. 30, 1918	Lenin wounded in assassination attempt by a right-wing Socialist-Revolutionary party member
Sept. 1918	Institutes "Red Terror" campaign of persecution and intimidation against enemies of revolution
Jan. 21, 1924	Lenin dies, aged 53, in Gorki of a cerebral hemorrhage

Index

John Haney graduated from London University in 1976 with an honors degree in classics. Between 1977 and 1981 he worked as a recording and performing artist with a contemporary music ensemble, regularly touring the United States and Europe. A resident of New York since 1982, he now works as an editor, writer, and lyricist. He spends most of his spare time studying the history of Soviet Russia. He is also the author of *Attlee* in the Chelsea House series WORLD LEADERS—PAST & PRESENT.

Arthur M. Schlesinger, jr., taught history at Harvard for many years and is currently Albert Schweitzer Professor of the Humanities at City University of New York. He is the author of numerous highly praised works in American history and has twice been awarded the Pulitzer Prize. He served in the White House as special assistant to Presidents Kennedy and Johnson.

PICTURE CREDITS

AP/Wide World Photos: pp. 69, 104, 106; The Bettmann Archive: pp. 15, 25, 37, 42, 50, 76, 82, 90, 92, 93, 103; Culver Pictures: pp. 29, 101; German Information Center: p. 17; David King Collection: pp. 38, 39, 40, 41, 48, 54; SNARK/Art Resource: pp. 18, 19, 68, 89, 105; Sovfoto: pp. 2, 12, 14, 16, 20, 22, 24, 26, 27, 28, 31, 32, 34, 35, 36, 45, 46, 52, 58, 61, 62, 64, 65, 66, 67, 74, 77, 79, 81, 84, 85, 86, 88, 94, 95, 96, 97, 98, 100, 102, 107; Sygma: pp. 44, 49, 50, 51, 55, 56, 57, 59, 60; UPI/Bettmann Newsphotos: pp. 78, 96